Rock Climbing for Beginners

A Complete Beginner's Guide to Mountaineering

By
Sam A Connelly

Table of Contents

Just for you

A Free Gift to our readers

Visit this link

https://www.samaconnelly.com/perfect-adventure.pdf

Joining the WA Community

Looking to live your dreams by having the best adventures and meeting other fun lovers like you? If so, then check out the Wild Adventurers (WA) Community here:

https://www.facebook.com/groups/173808284952610/

Introduction

- Are you bored doing nothing exciting and looking for a new hobby to spend your free time productively?
- Do you love the excitement of conquering challenges and working your way to success?
- Are you the adventurous type who loves to explore outdoor activities and try a new sport or hobby?

For you, a heart-throbbing activity that is too risky and dangerous can be the kind of sport that adds more value to how you spend your time, facing the challenge presented before you.

If you find yourself among them, you are lucky enough to have picked up this book among the many to choose from. It would be safe to describe you as the adventurous type who won't settle for anything less than an active and vibrant life. Rock Climbing or Mountaineering could be the perfect sport to breathe life into you when you feel that life becomes boring and unproductive.

For a rock-climbing enthusiast, there's no turning back or looking anywhere but up. Your constant goal is to reach the mountain summit. For each step on your way to the top, your determination gets stronger as you cling hard to your lifeline.

You are very much aware that you need to focus on the cold, rocky surface standing before you. It seemed too scary and enormous to conquer, but there's no turning back. Tiny drops of perspiration embed your forehead, and you can feel them running down your spine and to your legs before settling on your soles.

Your eyelashes try to redirect the tiny stream of sweat originating from your damp forehead to protect your line of vision before traversing across your entire body while your hands tremble as your palms search for the next hold to grab. The search for a foothold follows, and the same process is repeated for your other hand and foot. With every move, your cells cry out in agony, and you fight against your mind and body. Your energy subsides in each step but is quickly renewed as your mind attempts to dwell on the challenge. The thought of the top is what keeps you going.

The upward journey is indeed scary for someone new to rock climbing, but as you reach the top and are welcomed by a blast of refreshing sensation, a realization hits you hard. ROCK CLIMBING is not just a sport or a hobby. It's the ULTIMATE SELF-CHALLENGE

– a life-changing adventure that trains and disciplines your mind and body for SUCCESS!

Rock climbing is a confidence boost that keeps you coming back for more and leads to a fast improvement in the shortest possible time. The enthusiasm and satisfaction of climbing a mountain and conquering your fear of heights without actually failing will make you strive to level up every time you do it again. Each effort drives you to maximum performance for self-improvement. Acquiring the ability to quickly reap the benefits of going through such an intense activity makes rock climbing a perfect sport for those who want instant-driven rewards.

While Rock Climbing benefits both body and mind, basic preparations and safety measures are essential to a beginner's success. Rock Climbing would use your body from top to bottom; therefore, it is necessary to condition every muscle, bone, and entire body. In desperate times, every cell in your body seems to work together to achieve one GOAL – to reach the top!

Rock Climbing for Beginners is designed specifically for active people looking for a new hobby or adventure for more productive use of their free time. If you are particularly interested in mountain climbing but don't know how to get started, then you're lucky to have picked up this book. Reading this handy guide will bring you more benefits than you ever imagined.

This definitive guide will walk you through your first adventurous climb and provide you with the necessary skills and knowledge to make this journey safe – from mindset to body positioning and many more! Here's just a fraction of what you will learn from this essential guide:

- Climbing techniques
- Knots and anchors
- Bouldering and traditional climbing
- Device and safety checks
- Mountaineering Training
- And many more!

About the Author

My name is Sam A Connelly, and I'm an adventurous hobbyist who has spent more than a decade of my life rock climbing and training sports enthusiasts to develop good climbing skills and achieve their long-term desire for climbing.

Every time people ask why I had chosen rock climbing as my hobby and sports, my usual answer would be:

"The thought of reaching the summit equates to conquering a big challenge, and it makes me feel unstoppable. Imagine what it takes to max out your energy and enthusiasm to prove to yourself that you can do it? Once you do, you can assess and accept the risks of failure and progress like there are no doubts you would succeed in anything you do – the skills, the drive, and the resilience to overcome obstacles and failures. Climbing gave me all these."

My long years of experience in rock climbing did not only provide me the confidence to drive myself further every time I achieved my goal. It also developed in me the passion for sharing my experiences with other people. I want you to believe more in yourself and in whatever you do – to reach the summit and reach the peak of your life – the fulfillment of your goals and dreams. This passion drove me to write this book, **"Rock Climbing: A Complete Beginner's Guide to Mountaineering,"** with the end goal of helping others achieve what they want in life.

Having used techniques that drive results, I am confident that readers can acquire the same benefits I gained through this experience in mountain climbing. What made me sure to write this book was on-site training and a well-rounded lifestyle, which you are about to learn from the book based on real-life adventures.

Helping others gain knowledge and skills in rock climbing and mountaineering is my ultimate goal in life and legacy to all reading this book.

If you want to achieve what I had reached and gained, including the full benefit of knowing what it means to push yourself to the top, **GRAB A COPY OF THIS ESSENTIAL GUIDE**, and start living a life that you truly desire.

Chapter 1: Start Climbing

In every sport or hobby, preparation is significant to your success. Mountaineering is not an exception to this and is even much more demanding than other activities. Ascending a mountain requires you to be physically fit and have adequate experience with a variety of terrain.

Preparation for mountain climbing involves training your body and ensuring that you have the technical skill for a safe journey to the summit. It would be best if you also prepared your mind for challenges along the way, and on top of everything, you need to equip yourself for your combat with gravity as you push yourself up at high altitudes.

It may be far beyond your comfort zone, but as long as you're equipped to fight against all hurdles, mountaineering can quickly be learned by anyone. Training is an essential aspect of mountain climbing. If you're generally healthy, determined, resilient, trainable, and willing to put a lot of effort into your success, mountaineering can be the best experience you can have.

How to Prepare for Climbing

There are two main types of mountaineering.

- Alpine Style
- Expedition Style

The most common type and famous is the Alpine style which involves a simple, straightforward climb. In this type of climb, you don't need the use of supplemental oxygen and high-altitude porters.

Conversely, the expedition-style involves having a fixed-line of stocked camps along the way and requires expedition staff to travel up and down to set up camps and do some rope checking and fixing.

As part of your preparation for mountain climbing, setting up your goal is essential. Achieving a climb beyond your current fitness level can be very challenging, and therefore, you need a training plan that can push you further than what you have achieved so far.

Regardless of the mountaineering style, proper training is required in both types of mountaineering, especially when your goal involves climbing challenging peaks or multi-day trips.

A number of factors that will affect how much you need to train like:

- How long will you stay at a high altitude?
- How many days will it take you to climb?
- Will you need to train on any new skills?
- What pieces of equipment will you need to prepare for the journey?

Regardless of what type of climb you will be doing, still, you have to consider the following factors as they are all critical and must be fundamental to your mountaineering preparation:

- Altitude
- Ascent
- Cardio

Physical conditioning is vital for a faster and stronger motion for longer climbs while carrying a heavy load. It also helps improve resiliency while at rest.

For both experienced and inexperienced mountaineers, using the services of local professional guides is recommended to ensure safety and efficiency. These local guides have the best knowledge of the geographical setting that will help you navigate through challenging terrains. However, having a guide to assist you does not mean getting away with the training. They are there to support you but can't do things you have to do on your own.

Planning Your Training Schedule

Before your climb, you must at least undergo eight weeks of training to ensure that your fitness levels can deal with the upcoming challenges. However, it would be best if you did not fail to consider the difficulty of the journey and the length of your climb. It is best recommended that you start training early for long expeditions with challenging terrains.

It is essential to stick to a strict training regimen. You need to have your physical exercises and training sessions at least three times a week. For easy training, consider breaking down your training schedule into phases.

INITIAL PHASE – Physical Fitness

In the initial stage of your training, you must concentrate on general fitness. This phase may be easy for sports and bodybuilding enthusiasts or those who are into regular workouts. However, for those who are not much into doing vigorous exercises, this phase will prepare your body to make some adjustments to adapt to the new exercise regimen. Remember to incorporate in your training both cardiovascular fitness and motor fitness exercises.

PHASE TWO – General Uphill Training

Once your body gets used to cardio and motor skills exercises, take your training to a higher level. It's time to start training for uphill territory – e.g., specifically mountaineering like long hikes and climbs. To test your comfort levels, try to include a broad range of hill walks and minor peaks in your training.

PHASE THREE – Practice Similar Climbs

Before getting into your mountain climbing, try practicing climbs similar to your goal. It means, practice in an environment with the same weather conditions while carrying the same load and doing expended climbs for endurance testing. In short, do a mock climbing to give it a try.

Things to Include in Your Training

Working out several times a week can prepare you for any peak to prepare for the climbing challenge ahead. Having scheduled training will also mentally prepare you. However, be sure that you keep everything in balance to avoid any injury and leave enough time for recovery. Balance is indeed crucial to your success which is why training is greatly emphasized in this guide.

Consider the following areas to focus on to attain balance.

Cardio Training

Cardio exercises are essential to improve your overall fitness – including your heart and lungs. When preparing for mountain climbing, you have to work to improve these two major body organs. Aerobic exercises can get your heart pumping and regulate your oxygen levels. Here are some cardio exercises to keep your heart and lungs moving and in tune with your mountaineering activities.

- Cycling
- Hiking
- Boxing
- Dancing
- Trampolining
- Swimming Running
- Brisk walking
- Rowing
- Boxing

Another cardio-vascular workout to consider is the Cross fit training which incorporates strength and body conditioning.

As you move further into different phases of your training regimen, try cardio exercises every week. Build your training over time by starting with shorter workouts and progressing into longer and harder ones.

Interval Training

Another important aspect of your training is interval training which proves to maximize the cardiovascular benefits. Interval exercises will make your heart stronger while improving your anaerobic threshold. Involved in this type of workout is a series of high-intensity ones interspersed with relief periods.

While at rest, you can recharge your energy and improve your overall performance with a short burst of intense workouts.

Climbers benefit from interval training by gaining the ability to work at various paces. This method will help your heart increase its capability to pump blood throughout the body when done over a while. If you want to achieve the best out of interval training, do it for at least three months at a three-day interval.

Strength and Endurance

You will be carrying backpacks for the two types of mountaineering, especially for alpine-style mountaineering, as there will be no porters. Therefore, it is essential to do workouts that target areas that will have to bear the brunt of the load to build up your endurance. Increase strengths in all major leg muscles and core muscles. Because you will be putting strain on your body for an extended period, core exercises are beneficial. Working out these muscle groups will improve your balance as well.

Another thing you must not forget in planning your exercise regimen is flexibility, which is why stretching daily is a must. Some climbers are even into yoga exercises to track flexibility, tone, and strength in one go.

Hiking

While preparing for your mountain climbing adventure, you must get used to the different weather conditions and terrain. Conquering mountain heights is more challenging compared to hiking in flatlands. The type of terrain varies significantly in mountain climbing, and you will be facing several challenges at different altitudes.

So, as you are nearing your scheduled mountain adventure, build up more challenging hikes and try to anticipate your most strenuous mountaineering in terms of elevation, the weight of the backpack load, and hours of exertion. Practicing at high altitudes can be beneficial.

Technical Skills Training

You incorporate technical skills into your training, including rope work, climbing, scrambling, and using different equipment. It is not enough to gain power, strength, and an improved cardiovascular system for mountaineering, but you also need to learn how to deal with the challenging parts of walking.

To improve your balance and toughen your muscles for climbing, you may start with indoor wall climbing and learn the basics of rope works. However, you must also gain experience in real rock climbing.

Mental Training

Finally, it's not only your physical fitness that is important in your preparation training. It would also help improve your mental stamina, which measures your confidence and resilience - a real make-or-break deal.

Setting goals and targets are a great way to train your mind. It would be best if you did consider your end goals and include that small objective that counts to the achievement of your end goals. These small milestones will help you maintain your momentum while training.

Yes, maintaining your momentum in training is the best way to prepare yourself for your Mountain Climbing endeavor. It is the reason why you need a training plan and why you need to stick to it. Mountain climbers must stay on track of everything to achieve their goals even when there are setbacks. Setbacks can always happen and having resiliency and a positive mindset is necessary to overcome obstacles.

Doing your training must be fun and exciting instead of strenuous or mind-numbing activities. So, make sure to choose workouts that you find exciting and enjoyable so you won't be losing your momentum. It is also better to train with a buddy and plan with many people who can motivate you. You may also hire a personal trainer at the gym. To prevent boredom, try variations on hiking locations for a good mix of terrain, views, and situational experiences, including indoor and outdoor.

Understanding Terminology

Every field of endeavor has an established set of jargon or terminology, and rock climbing, or mountaineering is not an exception to this. Any miscommunication could lead to an accident or even the death of someone. To avoid this, learn and understand some terms commonly used in mountaineering before engaging in this sport or activity. Here are some of them.

A figure of 8 Knot: A highly secure knot that tightens as it is loaded with weight and woven in the shape of "8". A climber uses this knot to secure them to the climbing rope via the harness.

Anchor: It refers to a fixed point of attachment in a climbing rope with bolts, runners, and slings

Approach: the route that climbers take to walk, run, or skip to the base of the climb.

Arete: The edge of the wall forms like an acute angle, such as the corner of a building.

Barndoor: It is when a climber swings away from the rock because of being unbalanced.

Belay: A device that locks itself around a rock and provides friction to the rope to help climbers support each other's weigh-in case of a fall.

Belay device: A mechanism that catches a climber in case of a fall. When used correctly, it locks the rope in place to prevent the climber from falling.

Belayer: is the person controlling the rope attached to a climber to protect them from a fall.

Beta: refers to information on the moves, holds, or sequence on a climb shared verbally or in a guidebook.

Bolt: is a solid metal ring drilled into the rock for protection on sport-climbing routes. It expands on the rock and is highly secure. Clipped on the bolts are quickdraws to provide an anchor to which a rope runs through.

Bolted Route is a route in sports climbing protected with pre-placed bolts screwed into the wall to serve as an anchor.

Bomb-Proof: A well-secured protection provided by an anchor.

Bouldering: A climbing that is close enough to the ground and is safe enough to do even without the use of ropes. You can do it on boulders or the base of high climbs. You may also use spotters on high-risk problems and laid pads on the ground for protection.

Bouldering Pad: A durable pad made of thick foam placed just below the bouldering problem to cushion the climber fall.

Cam: A spring device designed to fit into cracks in rocks to secure a climber's rope to the wall.

Carabiner: A spring metal connecting a climber to their protection

Chalk bag: is a bag carried by climbers to keep chalks and their hands dried when climbing. It is usually tied to the back of a climbing harness or at the back of a waist belt.

Chimney: is a vertical crack on a wall of rock that is wide enough to fit your whole body. By applying opposing force to the sides, climbers can climb the chimney with their feet and bodies on the other side.

Clean: the act of cleaning a route by removing all the protection placed by the lead climber. The next-in-line climber is responsible for cleaning the route as they climb or rappel down.

Crag: refers to the outdoor climbing area or the rock or cliff used for climbing.

Crimp: refers to a very small or thin climbing hold or a horizontal rock surface that provides just enough space for a climber to insert his finger to enable them to mount enough pressure for pushing forward.

Crux: It is considered the most challenging part of a rock and is usually the first part.

Dynamic Rope: a rope you can slightly stretch with applied force to absorb the impact of the fall.

Dyno: jargon for a dynamic movement of climbing from one hold to another. It requires an action that enables the climber not to touch the rock when making a leap or a lunge.

Edging: it is the act of placing one's weight on a very small or thin foothold by using the edges of their feet instead of the soles.

Fist Jam: climbers use this technique for upward movement and stability when a crack is wide enough to accommodate a climber's fist.

Flash: a newbie successfully ascends a route on their first attempt using only prior knowledge and beta as their guide.

Free solo climbing: With no ropes and a belay system for protection, and routes are often high enough to require safety devices, this way of climbing is high-risk.

Gri-gri: refers to the auto-locking safety devices designed to catch a climber's fall.

Gaston: A kind of grip which involves pushing a hold instead of pulling.

Hand jam: Used when cracks are small enough for a hand to fit. It is much smaller than a fist jam.

Harness: A device that connects a climber to the climbing rope and consists of belts and leg loops.

Heel hook: the act of placing your heel around the rock, especially in overhead rock climbing

Jug: It is an easy formation on a rock that allows a climber to have a comfortable grip. It is usually a favorite spot among climbers.

Layback: a climber's move when shifting weight from one side and creating enough tension to use a vertical hold or crack for an upward movement.

Lead: refers to the first person to ascend a route by lead climbing. They place their gear or clip onto pre-placed bolts as they climb.

Mantel: A climber uses this technique to get into a ledge by applying downward pressure with their hands to lift their body high enough to get their feet up onto the ledge too.

Multi-pitch: A long route that requires more than one length of rope for as the lead climber reaches the apex of a single pitch to anchor, then belaying the next climber and using the same rope to ascend to the second pitch, with the belayer anchored at the top of the first pitch.

Nut: a small wedge-shaped metal attached to the end of a wire and used to jam in cracks as a piece of protection on a trad route.

Off-width: refers to a crack that is about 4-10 inches in width. It is too wide for your fist to fit into but too narrow for your body.

Pitch: It refers to the measurement of a climber based on the length of their climbing rope, which is usually 30-1,000 feet.

Pocket: A hole in a rock where you can insert a finger or two

Protection: Refers to a variety of devices required to protect a climber from falling a great distance. It includes nylon webbings, cams, bolts, and many others.

Rack: Necessary tools and devices required for the climb

Rappel: Also referred to as "abseil". It is the act of dropping down a cliff while holding on a fixed rope and mounting the leg against the rock. Mountain climbers usually use a belay device to maintain control.

Rope: referring to the climbing rope consisting of the sheath and core. The core is for rope strength, while the sheath is for a comfortable grip.

Climbing Grades

It's not enough to know how technically difficult it is to climb a mountain, but you also need to know how long it will take you to complete the course. Climbing grades suggest how long it will take for an experienced climber to complete the route.

- Grade I (About two hours)
- Grade II (About four hours)
- Grade III (About 4-6 hours)
- Grade IV (About one long day)
- Grade V (About two days, including an overnight stay)
- Grade VI (More than two days)

Major expeditions will be in Grade VII. Notice how Roman numerals are used in the grading to allow higher grades to be added in the future.

Regarding indoor climbing, grades aren't required because it is not a big deal to be stranded in the gym overnight.

Bouldering Grades

Have you ever heard someone say about doing a 5-point climb? The 5-point refers to the difficulty level, and they're using the Yosemite Decimal System (YDS). Although the YDS was initially designed for outdoor use, it is likewise used in climbing gyms to rate route difficulty.

Just like the difference in the U.S. and English Metric System, Australia, France, and Germany also have different rating systems. However, we will be using the U.S. rating, including the V Scale, used in the U.S. bouldering.

The Yosemite Decimal System (YDS)	
Route Classifications	
Class 1	Walking on a flat, easy trail that has long been established
Class 2	Hiking on a steep slope or scrambling, maybe hands are used in climbing.

Class 3	Climbing a steep hillside, moderate exposure, a rope may be carried but not used, and hands are used in climbing. A shortfall could be possible.
Class 4	Also, steep and exposed. People are using rope due to possible long falls.
Class 5	Because climbing is more technical, it requires belayed roping with a high potential of a fall which could be fatal. It is not advisable for novice climbers.

General Climbing Etiquette

It's time to deal with the etiquettes in climbing, and the local crag is not the same as your local gym. It would be best to observe specific rules of etiquette when climbing outdoors that don't typically apply in the gym environment. The ethics for responsible rock climbing or mountaineering are primarily unwritten, and it is for this reason that we have taken the time to write down a list of guidelines for you to observe as you start on your mountain climbing journey.

Generally, the climbing etiquette is based on the Leave No Trace Principles established by the Leave No Trace Center for Outdoor Ethics in the mid-80s and was implemented by:

- The US Force Service
- Bureau of Land Management
- National Park Service

Leave No Trace

It may sound like a thriller movie, but it pertains to the Seven No Trace Principles that a climber should aspire to while enjoying the outdoors. So whether you are hiking or rock climbing, don't forget to follow the LNT guidelines when you go outdoors.

Although the Seven Principles of Leave No Trace originate in backcountry settings, these principles can be applied anywhere - from the remote outback to local parks and almost every recreational activity.

Principle #1 – Plan Ahead and Prepare

Planning your trip is essential.

- It contributes to achieving climbing goals safely and enjoyably
- It allows you to leave no traces or damages to the wildlife
- It increases self-confidence and opportunities for knowing and establishing reconnections with nature
- It helps ensure the safety of climbers or mountain trekkers.

Bring all essentials for your activity such as water, climbing gear, food, chalk, etc.

Principle #2 - Travel and Camp on Durable Surfaces

Walk and camp on established trails and sites. If possible, avoid social trials.

Principle #3 - Dispose of Waste Properly

Seriously, you may be the typical climber who brings a lot of things with you. But when it's time to spread your items out, may it be because you are preparing your climbing gears or the food you eat, all those things end up in the ground at one point or the other, aware or unaware.

Try to keep all your belongings contained and organized to avoid the clutter and trash from spreading out. Consider the crag a shared space or your living room- it's commonplace for everyone, so keep it clean.

Yours or not, don't leave the trash, not only the non-biodegradable but the biodegradable items also like banana peels and apple cores. Dig a cat hole at least 200 meters away from trails, campsites, and water if you need to poop. Bury your used toilet paper thoroughly or pack it out in a plastic bag. Don't just leave it lying around.

Principle #4 - Leave What You Find

If you find something that amazes you, take a picture and leave it in its place.

Principle #5 - Minimize Campfire Impacts

The use of campfires was once a necessity and embedded in culture and history. There was a time when people couldn't think of camping without a fire. However, the appearance of natural environments is often degraded by the overuse of fires and the increasing demand for firewood. With the development of efficient camping stoves, campers were encouraged to shift away from the traditional fire for cooking. Camping beddings and garments were also designed for warmth, making them convenient and comfortable for campers.

Principle #6 - Respect the Wildlife

It's the home of our wild species - plants and animals. Give respect to their habitat. Do not disturb the wildlife, so wild animals are not scared. Keep away from wild animals. Disturbance can affect their ability to withstand the rigorous environment, so they travel quietly. An exception is when it is good to create a little noise to keep bears from scampering away from humans in bear country.

Touching and getting close to wild animals can be stressful to them. It is also possible that they harbor rabies and other diseases.

Principle #7 - Be Considerate of Other

You're not the only climber and person who enjoys the place. A critical element of outdoor etiquette is courtesy towards other visitors so that everyone can enjoy their outdoor experience. People reconnect to nature to listen through tranquility and solace. Excessive and distracting noises, unruly pets, and other things damaging to the surroundings may take away the natural appeal of the outdoors.

Climbing gyms may have blaring music, but good noise or music falls under this principle when it comes to outdoors. Remember to be considerate, especially when there are other people around.

Now, if you need to get psyched via loud music, plug in your headphones and minimize yelling. The point here is to be always considerate about the experience of others and not to go on tiptoes within climbing areas nor whisper when you speak to your friends.

In addition to these 7 Leave No Trace Ethical Principles that every climber must observe, we have other general etiquettes that you can add to your list.

Brush Off Tick Marks and Excess Chalk

An easily overlooked issue that could be overwhelming, unbrushed tick marks is another way of saying that you don't care about other future visitors in the area. Though tick marks are handy when climbing routes or boulder problems, they can be an eyesore and useless for the next climber who would have to brush off your tick marks. Spare them the hustle and do the work.

Tick marks also become problems for officials at highly regulated and prominent areas like Hueco Tanks. Chalk markings on rocks are an aesthetic issue for both climbers and non-climbers. So, it would be better to make your visual impact minimal. Please do not wait until all climbers lose their climbing privileges.

Respect the Local Ethics

Different areas impose different sets of ethics, and it also goes the same with rock climbing. To be precise, it wouldn't guarantee you that particular acceptable behavior in one area will also be permitted in another as it may be utterly absurd to them.

Let's say, in Fontainebleau (the bouldering birthplace); climbers have been labeling the problems for decades due to colored paints. Now, if you think it is acceptable anywhere and did it to the alpine gneiss in Rocky Mountain National Park, for sure, the climbing community will shun you for good, and the park service will shut down rock climbing.

Though there are no written ethics rules in climbing areas, visiting climbers can still know the dos and don'ts in a particular site. Just ask a few questions from a local before you go climbing. Respect local rules.

Adhere to All Official Rules and Regulations

Mostly, climbers end up climbing state or federal lands. Usually, you can find out rules and regulations on these lands posted online, at trailheads or visitor centers. When you follow these rules and regulations thoroughly, you can keep your reputation as a steward of the land as a climber.

Public land rock climbing is a great privilege that should not be taken for granted. But because of carelessness and foolishness, you could suffer the consequence of losing your climbing access to such areas. Reading and understanding the general rules of the lands that you visit is a must.

Chapter 2: Types of Climbing

Climbing pertains to an upward movement, ascending a steep surface. Nowadays, the term is getting a more popular definition— a challenging recreational activity.

Many people are fascinated with this activity as it challenges both mind and body. Climbing involves several sub-disciplines, techniques, settings, equipment, and different difficulty levels due to a broad spectrum of natural formations worldwide.

As someone new to rock climbing, it is always wise to be equipped with the proper knowledge and techniques, for there are many aspects of this activity that can be considered risky and extreme.

But before we delve deeper into the marvelous world of climbing, let's get acquainted with its various types. Here are the most popular ones:

Top Roping

The climbing rope has already been set up in top-roping — the rope threads through an anchor placed at the top of the climbing wall. One end of the rope is connected to the climber while the belayer holds on the other end. It's the belayer's job to take up the slack as the climber ascends the route.

Real top-roping requires the belayer at the top of the climbing wall, controlling the rope as the climber ascends. However, the widespread practice involves belayers situated on the ground level, with the anchor serving as a tool to make their assistance more effective. Because of this setup, the practice is also known as BOTTOM-ROPING.

Getting Started

Before starting with the outdoors, you will likely have to spend time training in a gym to hone your skills.

Climbing is both a physical and mental activity that demands a lot of practice, technical knowledge, and patience. Practicing in a climbing gym is a superb way to improve these said traits. A lot of gyms offer certified instruction on gear, leading, and shifting to outdoor climbing.

If your target is outdoor top-roping, the most sensible step to take is bouldering. It is the quickest method to grasp what rock climbing is. Besides, bouldering is an efficient method to build climbing strength and without the pressure of commitment. It is the best introduction for any rock-climbing neophyte.

Once your climbing strength is sufficient, you can start learning the basic top-roping—tying yourself in to climb and top-rope belay. And for this, you will have to attend a belay class.

Outdoor Top Rope Climbing

Although the setting differs, you will use the same kind of gear in both indoor and outdoor top-rope climbing. However, top outdoor roping is riskier simply because you have less control over the environment. But then again, the changes in scenery, terrain, and weather are all elements that add to the fun factor of outdoor top-rope climbing.

In an outdoor environment, there are two ways to set up top-rope climbing. First, the climber has to hike up to the top of the wall and perform one of these three methods:

- Anchor the rope to a large, sturdy tree.
- Construct the traditional anchor to run the rope through.
- Thread the rope through a pre-established bolted anchor.

Second, they have to allow a lead climber to ascend the rough and set up a bolted or traditional anchor.

Once the rope is secured through an anchor, you can hike back to the bottom and commence top-roping the route. If you let a lead climber do the setup, all you have to do is follow them up on top rope after they go back to the ground. In case that the route is overhanging or deviates a lot, make sure to climb on the end of the rope nearest to the wall.

To be on the safe side— if you're not yet confident about properly setting up an outdoor top-rope anchor, don't hesitate to ask someone to do it for you. Even if it's an easy skill to learn, the slightest mistake can cause severe injuries.

Reasons to Try Top Rope Climbing

Top roping may not be devised to get you to the highest peak of a mountain. However, it guarantees fun and enjoyment with your friends.

- ### Top Roping is Less Risky

Injuries happen in any climbing activity or sport. However, they are less likely to occur in top-roping compared to any other methods of rock climbing.

In top-rope climbing, belayers always keep the rope rigid, so top climbers will merely experience low rope-stretch falls. Consequently, top-roping is also the best option for any climber who aims to practice climbing without taking the fear of falling into concern too much.

- ### Top Roping Entails Less Technical Knowledge

New climbers only need to know to learn one new knot, and they can already start climbing.

The belaying for top roping is more straightforward than other climbing types since all the climber needs is to control the slack as the climber ascends.

- **Top Roping Helps Boost Muscle Coordination**

Although top roping is less demanding than other rock climbing types, the fact remains that climbers need to take on challenging moves and routes. And to complete these routes efficiently, one has to achieve good intramuscular coordination.

During top-roping, a climber simultaneously utilizes different muscle groups that enable them to pull their body up.

Sport Climbing

Sport climbing is a type of rock climbing wherein a permanent gear secures the climber. It is also a form of lead climbing since the climbing rope begins at the bottom, and the climber (known as the lead) clips in as they ascend the route. It makes sport climbing the opposite of top-roping, where the rope is hung at the top of the climbing wall or cliff.

History of Sport Climbing

In the United States, Smith Rock in the Oregon State Park is the birthplace of sport climbing, thanks to Allan Watts and his crew. They systematically bolted the routes on rappel and performed top roping moves before freeing them. While this may be the norm nowadays, it was a highly criticized practice back then.

In 1986, the famous French climber Jean-Baptiste Tribout helped cement the status of sport climbing with his feat in THE TO BOLT OR NOT TO BE route.

Climbing gyms absorbed the concept of sport climbing during the late 1980s, and both gyms and sport climbing became extremely popular during the 1990s.

Sport Climbing Preparation

Sport climbing, like any rock climbing, requires preparation. Although some may merely dismiss it just like any other form of rock climbing, the nuances and technicalities in this sport can be pretty surprising. Hence, it's crucial for any individual who wants to immerse in the world of sport climbing to find an experienced mentor.

Chances are, you already know who this person might be. After all, anyone who desires to try sport climbing has already tried indoor or gym climbing. It's crucial to familiarize yourself first with the basics of gear handling and safety precautions before venturing to sport climbing.

A sport climbing mentor will teach you to lead climbing, rappelling, lead belaying, cleaning anchors, and hanging quickdraws at a minimum. If you're lucky enough, they will teach you some "secrets," which you should take close to heart.

Sport Climbing Grades

Route grading systems differ by country. However, the two most common come from France and the United States.

The French grading system is widely used in Europe. The difficulty increases with the rise of numbers (1 to 9), letters (a to c), and the plus sign symbol (6a+, 6b+, 7a+, 7b+).

The United States of America is using the Yosemite Decimal System, which runs from 5.0 to 5.15d (the latest). Unfortunately, the grades aren't always consistent, even with the decimal system in the US. Typically, grades are approximately uniform in one area but radically differ between various areas. For instance, a 5.9 at Rifle may drastically go against the 5.9 of New River Gorge.

Also, it may surprise you that outdoor grades do not match the grades used in the gym. You will experience entirely different grading conventions in outdoor climbing, in this case, sport climbing. Remember that grading can be less formulaic and controlled in outdoor climbing, which makes outdoor climbs more challenging at a specified grade.

French	YDS
2	5.0
2+	5.1
3	5.2
3+	5.3
4a	5.4
4b	5.5

4c	5.6
5a	5.7
5b	5.8
5c	5.9
6a	5.10a
6a+	5.10b
6b	5.10c
6b+	5.10d
6c	5.11a/ 5.11b
6c+	5.11c
7a	5.11d

7a+	5.12a
7b	5.12b
7b+	5.12c
7c	5.12d
7c+	5.13a
8a	5.13b
8a+	5.13c
8b	5.13d
8b+	5.14a
8c	5.14b
8c+	5.14c

9a	5.14d
9a+	5.15a
9b	5.15b
9b+	5.15c
9c	5.15d

Note: French and Yosemite Decimal System don't always align like the chart above, but it will show you how they are usually compared.

Sport Climbing Etiquette

While gyms may have their respective set of written rules, outdoors have their unspoken ones. There are two essential things you must adhere to when doing sport climbing: RESPONSIBLE STEWARDSHIP and FELLOWSHIP. These two are the backbone of silent rules in outdoor climbing.

Do not:

- Break local or wilderness ethics, restrictions, closures, or waivers. Respect the environment where you do outdoor climbing since your future access depends on your behavior.
- Leave garbage anywhere. It's the basics and a sign of respect to both the environment and your fellow climbers. Do not leave food wrappers, tape shreds, or worse, human waste on the site.
- Be too loud. Shouting, laughing out loud, and playing loud music can distract other climbers. Be mindful and considerate of them.
-

- Let your pet spoil the fun for others. Crag dogs, if poorly behaved, can be a source of stress and headache to other climbers. Make sure that your dog is well-behaved before bringing it to the crags.
- Top rope on any fixed hardware. Conventions vary in different areas, but this one is a big "NO!" The hardware is there for cleaning and not facilitating your top-rope moves.
- Take quickdraws or fixed hardware because it's plain stealing. Feel free to use a hanging quickdraw if somebody left it. What you are not allowed to do is to take it as your own.
- Discard a gear or rope on a route you are not climbing.

Do:

- Organize your things. Try to contain your items as much as you can.
- Be kind and patient. Crags are places to enjoy and learn more about your interest. It would be best to keep it a warm place where happiness is shared. Do not embarrass or isolate other climbers, especially those who are pretty new to the sport.
- Wipe off markings. Don't just leave them there; erase the markings you make when you're done.
- Be friendly and communicative. Be transparent and open about your intentions, as this will encourage everyone to do the same. You can also share information, the wall, or gear to show your goodwill.

Speed Climbing

As the name suggests, speed climbing is a form of indoor rock climbing with speed as the climber's ultimate goal. It is also known as a discipline of competitive climbing that an individual or a team can do.

Climbers use their hands and feet for grip, pulling themselves up with straight arms. This method enables them to achieve their maximum speed as they move upwards or downwards while never losing momentum.

Speed climbing can be traced back to its origins in Soviet Russia in the 1940s, wherein the climbers' scores are measured by the time it took them to complete the routes. Competition between two parties was quite common among Soviet climbers back then. In 1976, the Soviets introduced the first-ever international speed climbing competition in the Russian city of Gagra.

Meanwhile, modern speed climbing is a head-to-head battle for the fastest time on a fifteen-meter climbing wall with identically designed vertical routes. Speed climbers spend years mastering the discipline that can diminish fractions of a second from their time.

Since speed climbers rely on pulling their weight up with their arms, they must undergo special training for developing their upper body. It likewise provides them the advantage over other competitors who may have more developed upper body muscles than they have.

Those who want to stay physically fit enjoying the thrill of an adventure can try speed climbing. It's also a perfect activity for anyone looking to challenge themselves or overcome their fear of heights.

Traditional Climbing

Traditional climbing, also known as *trad climbing*, is the oldest type of competitive climbing. It emerged as a separate discipline from sport climbing in the 1980s. Compared to sport climbing which focuses on physical challenges, traditional climbing commands both physical and mental prowess.

Traditional climbing requires carrying and placing protection such as climbing cams, chocks, and other devices instead of clipping protection into pre-assembled bolts. Traditional climbers must also have adequate technical knowledge of climbing anchors and the skill of creating them.

Traditional climbing is often done outdoors on natural climbing rocks where there are no pre-placed bolts.

When it comes to grading, the United States uses the Yosemite Decimal System. Meanwhile, the United Kingdom has its dedicated traditional grading system called, *The British Trad Grading System*, divided into two parts—the *adjectival* and *technical* grades.

The adjectival grade, marked from Diff to E10, provides an overall picture of the route. It includes how sustained, protected, and difficult the course is.

The technical grade, marked from 4a to 7b, pertains to the difficulty of the most challenging single move performed on a route.

History of Traditional Climbing

The earliest known climbing forms as a sport are still under debate as no evident records show that climbing was considered a sport. By the end of the 1800s and the dawn of the 1900s, people started rock climbing for fun, not solely for survival. Places such as the Elbe area in Germany, the Dolomites in Italy, and England became favorites of climbers. During the following decades, climbing strictly went up the rock face using equipment and placing bolts en route for protection.

As climbing developed into a sport around the 1970s and 1980s, rock climbing has expanded to several disciplines. Traditional climbing became a distinguished form of rock climbing in the 1980s due to some climbers who identified themselves as more formal.

Trad climbing retained its core despite the constant innovation of protective gears and equipment. It is most prevalent in the United States, where larger rocks are formed. For instance, Utah and Yosemite have been dubbed traditional climbing meccas.

Getting Started

Before taking off to the rocks and hills with your climbing devices, you must know how they work— that's given. You also have to find a seasoned climbing instructor and make solid anchors and place protection.

You have to spend time on the ground and assess the necessary aspects before climbing the cliff. Consider how to fit the cams, hexes, and wedges into varying rock features.

Different rock formations call for other gear pieces employed in an assortment of methods. Because of this, you have to gain confidence in your equipment and broad knowledge about them.

Types of Traditional Climbing

As mentioned above, traditional climbing has evolved, and some groups of climbers realize the differences in their form from that of other fellow trad climbers.

Below are some samples of still-valid forms of traditional climbing:

> ➢ **Big Wall Climbing**

As the name suggests, this form requires climbers to climb a massive wall. Many consider big wall climbing as the most challenging yet exciting form of traditional climbing. How? First, the climber might be forced to use their equipment since there is an excellent chance that the entire route is not bolted. Secondly, this might mean that the climber would be climbing a collective of pitches, most likely over a couple of days. Since we're talking about an actual traditional climber here, they would have to survive for the entire time without rappelling down for supplies (i.e., gear, water, and food) and ascending again afterward. Moreover, they should never leave anything behind, specifically trash and refuse, on the wall.

> ➢ **Bolted Climbing**

Generally, trad climbing is unbolted, and all protection is placed on lead, although its earlier forms involved the climbers bolting the route as they go. Some traditional courses, particularly the older ones, already have bolts on. It's up to climbers whether they use those bolts or opt to use something else.

Some people don't consider bolted climbing as another form of traditional climbing. Some even argue that using pre-placed bots is cheating. However, since these preset bots are scarce and infrequent, many still believe that bolted climbing is another type of trad climbing.

> ➢ **Crack Climbing**

Crack climbing is getting more popular in the US, and many consider it the "ultimate fighting with a rock."

Crack climbing is typically unbolted; thus, it requires climbers to put the gear on the lead to protect themselves in the process. By this, crack climbing makes it yet another form of traditional climbing.

Bouldering

Many consider Bouldering the simplest form of climbing as it only requires chalk, a pair of climbing shoes, and crash pads. It is also practiced at indoor walls, small rocks, boulders, or artificial exterior bouldering walls. Ropes are unnecessary for this activity since the climbers don't need to climb very high and jump back down.

History of Bouldering

No one can point out where Bouldering originated, but many believe it started in the Lake District, United Kingdom, and Fontainebleau, France. These two areas are abundant in sandstone boulders sitting in the middle of the forests and were the grounds where the term BLEAUSARDS or more popularly known as "boulderers."

Bouldering got two new forms of training tools in the 1980s. First, the climbing gyms and indoor Bouldering helped develop the sport in artificial settings. It also enables boulderers to train constantly regardless of the weather, climate, or season. The second is called CRASH PADS or BOULDERING MATS. This tool helps absorb the shock during the climber's fall, protecting them from bad falls and injuries. Boulderers can also venture to new climbing routes and terrains that were formerly deemed high-risk.

Bouldering is still growing in popularity all over the world, particularly in Europe and the United States. Since many people have shifted their interest in Bouldering, it's only reasonable to establish a system that aids climbers in identifying the difficulty of a boulder problem before trying them. Two primary grading scales are in use today, the FONT SCALE and the V SCALE. The first is widely used in Europe while the latter is popular in North America.

John Gill, an American mathematician, devised the Font Scale (short for FONTAINEBLEAU SCALE), which uses the open-ended numerical system, ranging from 1 to 9A.

The second one, John "Verm" Sherman's V SCALE (also known as the HUECO SCALE Was developed in the 90s at Hueco Tanks State Historic Site. The difficulty ranges from V0 to V17, although the system is open-ended. VB is sometimes used for problems easier than V0. Sometimes, issues are post-fixed with + (for more difficult ones) or – (for easier ones) to determine the difficulty range within a single grade.

Reasons to Try Bouldering

Bouldering presents several benefits for your general well-being, and these include:

- **Physical and Mental Improvement**

Bouldering does not merely guarantee a full-body workout but also mental exercises. It requires the mobilization of your entire body — not merely your arms or upper body — to complete the route.

Bouldering helps boost core strength, balance, and flexibility. In the beginning, you might not feel the difference, but you will get the after-effects gradually from your shoulders, abs, and lower limbs. Aside from these, your finger grip will immensely get stronger.

With Bouldering, your brain also has the opportunity for a workout. It improves your focus as you complete each challenge along the route you take, and you will realize it leaves no space for distractions or idle thoughts. Moreover, Bouldering allows you to dispense stress as you burn off calories, leaving you refreshed and reinvigorated by the end of the day.

- **Interconnection With People**

Bouldering is a community sport as you have to work with other boulderers to figure out routes together. You also gain the opportunity to meet other people from different backgrounds and statuses in life. This setting differs from the likes of rope-climbing, wherein climbers are spread out across separate lanes. In Bouldering, you have to give and take since some routes extend over others. When this happens, you can exchange ideas and tips with your fellow boulderers.

Bouldering aids in breaking down boundaries as you can start a conversation or interaction without feeling awkward. Instead, you almost instantly share a feeling of camaraderie because of your common interest and hobby.

On the fun side, if you're fond of sharing something about your life on social media, Bouldering can help you with this endeavor. You can take fantastic photos and videos of your graceful climbing.

- **Problem-Solving**

Bouldering allows you to enhance your problem-solving skills as it trains you to undertake physical challenges that require figuring out solutions as you move along the route. Think of it as an equation, but a lot more fun.

The sport opens you to explore a lot of probabilities to complete a route, depending on your body type, skills, and abilities. Tackling the challenges often varies from person to person since everybody is unique.

The essential aspect of Bouldering is learning how to place your body weight. Hence, if you want to improve at Bouldering, you must hone your skills and techniques, such as mastering footwork and strengthening finger grips.

Bouldering Basics

As a novice in Bouldering, knowing the fundamentals of Bouldering can at least help you minimize the perils connected with the sport:

Spotting

Bouldering necessitates SPOTTERS from time to time, especially when outdoors. The role of spotters involves guiding boulderers to a fall or preventing them from landing in an improper position that will cause injury.

When outdoors, a crash pad might not be adequate to cover the ground or spot where a climber touches down. With the guidance of a spotter, a climber can properly land as spotters will make sure that the climber won't fall out of the padded zone or land mistakenly on their head, neck, or shoulder.

Falling Properly

While bouldering walls are not as high as those in top-rope climbing still, you are most likely to fall and get injured, especially when you don't know how to carry it out properly. Your wrists and ankles are at the most risk of injuries, so you should find out how to keep your body relaxed to execute your landing correctly.

The essential technique is to distribute the landing force and impact across your entire body to steer clear from fractures. How do you do this? Typically, it would be to land on both your feet with your knees in a slightly bent position and then fall on your side or back. Make sure to keep your arms and hands close to your body. Landing with your arms stretched out will only result in injuries.

Bouldering requires you to bend in different strange positions sometimes. However, it is best to keep your body relaxed during your fall, and you will be okay.

Safety and Injury Prevention

Even though we may know about spotting and landing properly, it's still safe to know some guidelines on keeping ourselves safe and free of injury.

Bouldering contributes to higher injuries among the various forms of climbing due to several reasons. For one, boulder problems tend to demand more complex moves. Another one is that Bouldering requires no ropes, so falling is a given. Knowing how to execute proper falling merely reduces the probability of injuries.

To maximize safety, you must always do warm-ups. Do not forget to use climbing chalk to absorb all the moisture on your hands and finger tape to protect your fingers. When bouldering outdoors, make sure to work with a spotter and never forget to use crash pads.

Outdoor and Indoor Bouldering

Aside from the venue, how does indoor and outdoor Bouldering differ from each other?

Outdoor Bouldering in a natural setting means working on terrains with sandstone, limestone, granite, and volcanic rocks. When you go outdoor Bouldering, come prepared with your camping gear as well as bouldering tools and equipment such as:

- Brushes
- Chalk bag
- Mat
- Bouldering pad
- Skincare kit

These devices help you clean off debris such as dust, leaves, and soil that have been accumulated on the rocks.

You get to experience a much higher bouldering level in highball bouldering since it involves climbing boulders as high as 15 to 40 feet. Compared to normal Bouldering, highball bouldering involves more significant hazards and risks to both rookies and experienced climbers.

Bouldering gyms imitate the significant elements of outdoor Bouldering and make them accessible to boulderers throughout the year regardless of the weather and climate outdoors. Indoor gym bouldering features artificial climbing holds in various surfaces, colors, shapes, and sizes. It utilizes a color-coding system to categorize different routes. There are varying difficulties with each level and type of holds, such as jugs, pinchers, crimps, and slopers. These challenges help improve your grip and bouldering techniques.

Bouldering Etiquette

Bouldering has some unspoken etiquette that must be observed to make climbing a pleasant experience for everyone, whether outdoors or indoors.

Maintain Cleanliness and Orderliness

The crags you climb and the ground you tread upon are all part of the environment you enjoy. It is only reasonable to maintain the cleanliness of the area, even if it means clearing off the garbage of the previous climber. Trash is a health hazard as it can attract harmful pests and make the surroundings foul-smelling.

Keep Your Things Organized

Tidy up and organize your things to avoid unnecessary "attention" from other climbers who might be tempted to pick up something not theirs. However, should there be an instance when someone unintentionally mistakes your shoes for theirs, don't be too distressed about it.

Be Nice

It is a universal rule in any situation. Remember that Bouldering is a community sport. You share the walls, routes, and, at times, gears with other climbers. It would be awesome to be always willing to communicate and interact with your fellow boulders or climbers.

Be Considerate

Consider others who may also want to try the route you're trying. Do not hog the lane, especially when you're bouldering outdoors where many people may be queuing for their turn.

Don't Give Unsolicited Advice

Sometimes, your fellow boulderers don't like "spoilers." They prefer to learn as they go and finish their challenges without too many hints coming from others. Even if you mean well, don't readily give away tips unless they get stuck and ask you for advice.

Lead Climbing

Lead climbing is a more advanced technique compared to top-roping. Herein, the climber controls the rope themselves as they ascend, clipping it as they go up to their route. Unlike in top-roping, the rope here is not threaded through an anchor before the climber begins climbing.

The climber may clip into the QUICKDRAWS, consisting of carabiners that they can attach to the wall as they ascend the route. Meanwhile, the belayer needs to work using more advanced skills, ensuring that the climber has enough rope to reach and clip securely. They also have to keep in mind that they should only provide the right amount of rope to take in and keep extension to ensure the climber's safety and success.

Chapter 3: Apparatus and Equipment for Climbing

Rock Climbing is considered one of the most extreme sports nowadays. Both exhilarating and adventurous, one should have the right and necessary equipment before attempting to climb a mountain summit.

An excellent shape and proper technical training for mountaineering are necessary for a successful climbing experience. However, aside from these, you also need to have the essential adequate gear and clothing. Your equipment mainly depends on the trek you're undertaking, and if you're hiring a guide, some of these are probably available to rent, so make sure to check before making any purchases.

The Essential Gear and Equipment Rock Climbers Should Have

Listed below are the things you need so you can scale a cliff surface safely:

Anchor Equipment

Typically, you would want to climb a route equipped with chains and bolts. However, you will set up the anchor yourself from which you will hang your top rope. You will need a 25-feet, 7mm cordelette (that's the minimum) and at least four locking carabiners—two pieces each for the rope side and anchor side.

Backpacks

You will need a backpack to bring your full climbing gears easily and safely to your climbing area. You can use any backpack. However, consider choosing backpacks specially designed for climbing purposes with great features for storing ropes and gear.

Compared to your usual backpack, mountaineering backpacks have a sleeker and narrower design that allows uninterrupted arm movement. It also has side rope holders, crampon patches, and sleeping bag/tent holders. They also have hip belts that provide a secure hold whenever a mountaineer wears them.

Rope bags are also needed to avoid your climbing rope falling out in the dirt, eventually contributing to its degradation.

Belay Device

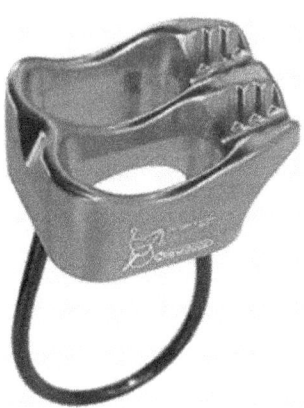

A belay device is a mechanical friction brake used by climbers to lower them from an ascent or prevent falling. Since it provides multiple friction points, the device doesn't have to hold the climber's entire weight as they descend.

A belay device is a mechanical friction brake used by climbers to lower them from an ascent or prevent falling. Since it provides multiple friction points, the device doesn't have to hold the climber's entire weight as they descend.

Choose what you prefer: tubular or assisted braking device. Just make sure that the carabiner you bought is designed for belay device use.

Carabiners

A carabiner is a simple device that prevents any attachments from detaching or getting removed. They are frequently used in connecting the climbing rope with other equipment such as cam devices, nuts, and bolts. These are usually made of solid steel that features a gate that will allow your rope or other small equipment to pass through. The gate feature contains screw threads that secure it in place once locked.

Mountaineering carabiners should mix locking and non-locking carabiner types used for building crevasse rescue hauling systems and rock anchors. Usually, a mountaineer brings at least five non-locking and four locking carabiners, which could increase in number depending on the trek they are planning to take.

Chalk and Chalk Bag

Like climbing shoes, climbing chalks are a necessity to mountain climbers. Climbing chalks allow climbers to increase grip and friction while holding onto a rock, preventing them from slipping. If you have sweaty palms or hands, you can also use the climbing chalk to avoid accidents during the climb. Make sure, however, to buy smaller-grained chalk whenever possible, along with a chalk bag that is pretty easy to open and close anytime.

Climbing Cams

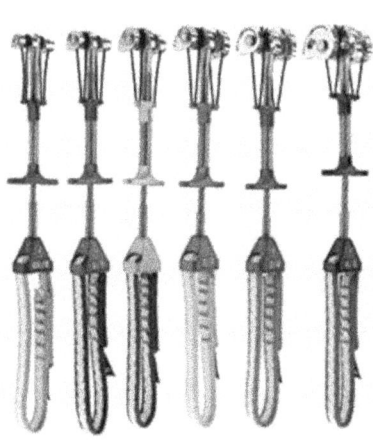

Spring-loaded cam devices or climbing cams are equipment that can easily fit and take a grip inside crags or cracks in between rocks. Cams are frequently used in instances wherein nuts and bolts won't work. Its primary feature is that the more a climber pulls on it, the farther the devices spread apart, securing its grip on the walls between the cracks. Unlike pitons and bolts, it doesn't damage the rocks it inserts itself to, making it an ideal and essential tool for ethical climbers.

Climbing Harness

Choose to purchase a harness that fits you well and one that has gear loops (for carrying equipment). Otherwise, you probably have one if you're a seasoned gym climber.

It would be best to have a harness with a ventilation feature, padding, extra-wide webbing, and moisture support. Make sure that your newly bought harness should work comfortably with your clothing to ensure a full range of movement. Since its primary function is to keep its wearer safe during the climb, examining the harness for damage or defects is necessary even when buying a new one.

Climbing Helmet

One of the much-needed items to prepare before you start is the climbing helmet. You must wear a helmet before climbing whether outdoor or indoor. It will protect your head in case of a fall or when falling rocks or debris are overhead. Purchase one that will fit you snugly yet comfortably to wear.

Like any other helmet, a climbing helmet's purpose is to protect your head from getting damaged or injured from falling rocks and debris during the climb as accidents can happen. Sometimes, rock pieces, dust, and other debris may fall on mountain climbers. However, wearing a durable climbing helmet can protect your head from serious injury in case of a falling event. When choosing your climbing helmet, make sure that it is not too small or too large for your head that it can obstruct your line of vision.

Unlike helmets used in rock climbing, mountaineering helmets are sturdier and have clips so that mountaineers can attach a headlamp to them. Some of them even have closable vents, a feature that is nice to have when climbing on cold and snowy terrains.

Climbing Ropes

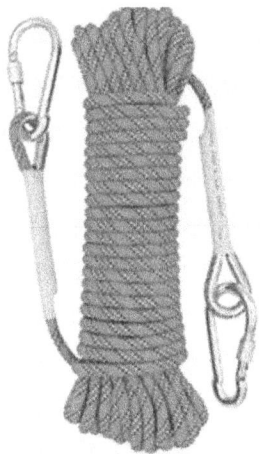

No mountaineer or rock climber attempts a climb without a rope. If you have a mountain guide, ropes are usually provided for free or for rental. Otherwise, you need to buy one for yourself. If you decide on buying one, make sure that you choose a lighter brand that still retains its durability to lessen your overall weight while climbing.

Ropes are essential pieces of rock-climbing equipment necessary for mountain climbing. There are only two instances wherein the rock climber doesn't need them. First is when they are free soloing, and second is when they are bouldering with a crash mat already set up for safety. When buying a rope, make sure to thoroughly check some factors, such as length, rope type, features, diameter, and safety ratings. Additionally, make sure that you bring just enough rope whenever you're climbing, so you won't have to bear the inconvenience of extra length and weight.

When buying a climbing rope, you also need an appropriate safety harness where you can link it. In choosing your harness, you need to consider what type of rock climbing you will use and how much money you are willing to spend. However, always keep in mind comfort and versatility as your priority.

Climbing Shoes

Trying to climb a wall without proper climbing shoes is simply unthinkable. To prevent skin abrasions, choose a pair of climbing shoes that properly fit you and are made of thin material that will allow your feet to breathe. Make sure that they have rubber soles

that can step securely on any surface without slipping and with grooves that will enable them to have enough grip between rocks and crags. However, buying the right climbing shoes depends on the user's experience or skill level. Although even the best shoes can't enhance your skill in mountain climbing, the best they can do is to secure your steps.

Climbing Tape

Climbing tapes prevent climbers from getting flappers, tears on climbers' finger pads that can occur whenever they slip off a hold. Some apply climbing tapes preemptively to prevent flappers from forming or putting them on to heal their flappers. Either way, it is a handy piece of equipment.

Crampons

Crampons are generally used when walking through snowy terrains and glaciers, crampons are built of either steel or aluminum. Steel types are required whenever you plan on climbing icy mountains with solid rock formations since it provides weight for added stability and is more durable. On the other hand, Aluminum types are recommended for moderate snow climbs since they are considerably lighter than steel.

Crash Mat

Frequently used by bouldering fanatics, crash mats prevent climbers from getting injured in a falling event by acting as a protective cushion. It is usually the only thing that prevents you from getting broken bones after falling on the hard floor below. However, remember that you need to buy the right crash mat depending on the type of bouldering that you want to do.

Crevasse Rescue Equipment

If you're planning to make some snowy and glacier trips, it is necessary to carry crevasse rescue equipment. A set consisting of lightweight pulleys, snow pickets, accessory cords, and slings is used in case you or a fellow climber happens to fall into a crag or a crevasse.

Headlamps

Headlamps are a must-have, whether you are mountaineering for just a day or a whole week. Most mountaineering attempts require enough lighting that doesn't require a hand for holding, hence the invention of headlamps. However, keep in mind to bring extra batteries for extended journeys.

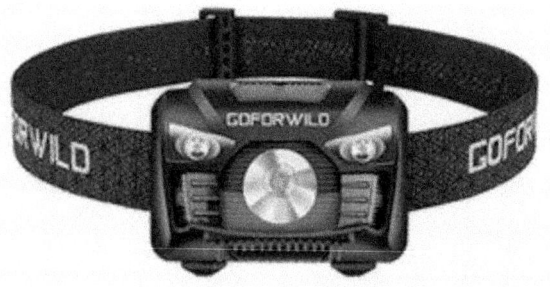

Hydration Systems

Water is a basic necessity, especially when you're mountain climbing, for you need to continuously hydrate, considering the heat and fatigue you need to go through. So, always remember to bring bottles of water with you.

Water is a number one necessity, especially when mountaineering since we need to rehydrate whenever we feel hot or thirsty. For this, you can either bring two wide-mouthed and rigid plastic bottles or a hydration reservoir and a storage bottle.

Ice Axe

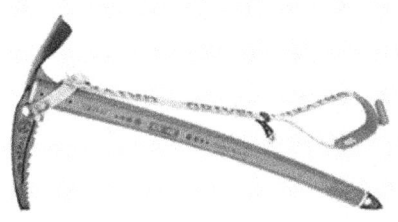

Ice axes are used in taking a good hold of icy mountain caps during the climb, one should consider their activity and size when looking for the right ice axes that will do the job. And take note, they always come in pairs.

Mountaineering Boots

A good pair of mountaineering boots will not only provide traction and foothold during the climb on rocky terrain; it must also have the ability to attach crampons when you need to travel through icy landscapes. Boots can either be insulated, suitable for snow and glacier climbs, or non-insulated, ideal for climbing in places with mild temperatures.

Mountaineering Harnesses

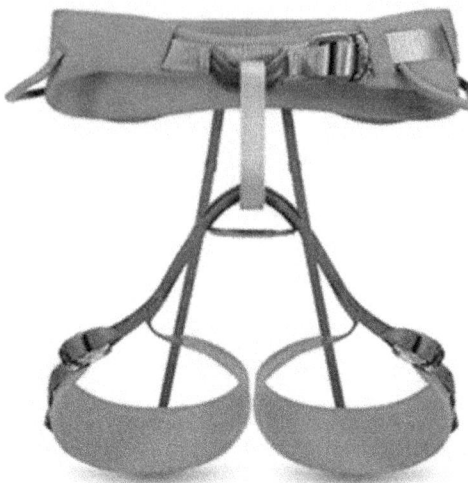

Compared to rock-climbing harnesses, mountaineering harnesses are more comfortable and convenient. They are usually flat webbing and have low-profile gear loops that keep the harness compact, comfortable, and lightweight. They also have leg loops that can be detached anytime whenever the mountaineer doesn't need them.

Quickdraws

Quickdraws are two pieces of carabiners attached by a textile sling. It allows carabiners to connect to two different pieces of equipment, mostly a bolt hanger on one end and a climbing rope on the other end. Its primary purpose is to prevent too much friction on the equipment by

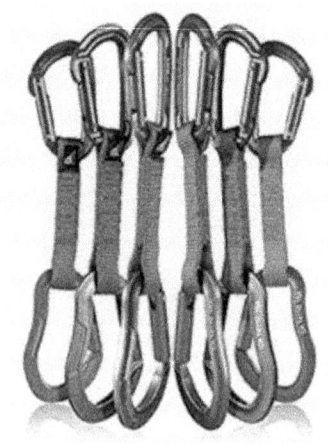

allowing basic movements. If you're planning to buy one, ensure that the textile sling that connects the carabiners has no cracks, tears, or any defect that might affect its durability.

Sleeping Bags

If you're doing an overnight climbing trip, bringing a sleeping bag with you should suffice.

Stove

Cooking your food or boiling your water is necessary when mountaineering, hence the need to bring a portable stove with you. Usually fueled by either butane or kerosene, you do not need to spend time trying to find dry firewood, which is impossible when you're in cold and icy terrain.

Tents

For mountaineering activities that take more than a day to complete, having a tent is necessary. Mountaineers usually take a three-season tent whenever they plan on mountaineering during hot and dry times. But, if you're planning on taking a snowy climb, taking a four-season tent with you is much better.

Water Treatment

If you're camping on a high mountain, you might need to obtain your water either from a river source or by melting enough snow. Most of the time, you need to boil then cool it first before using it to prevent microbes and harmful river  parasites from entering your body. However, if you do not want to constantly boil the water for fuel conservation purposes, you need to bring water treatment tools. It can be in the form of water filters, chlorine tablets, or ultraviolet purifiers.

Chapter 4: Knots and Anchor

Most people learn about knot tying during their scouting years but most likely forget before they reach adulthood. However, as climbers, these knots are a lifeline to them, no matter how simple or complicated they look.

Aside from knowing how to climb, a mountaineer will constantly work with a rope, so mastering it is necessary. Hence, one should learn how to tie knots, bends, and hitches the right way. But before doing anything, we must understand what a knot is, and other terms related to rope management.

Learning to tie knots and using them correctly is helpful during rock climbing or mountaineering and in everyday life. But before doing anything, we must understand what a knot is, and other terms related to rope management.

- **Knot:** is what is tied in a piece of webbing, string, or rope.
- **A bend**: is a kind of knot that joins two different ropes together.
- **Hitch:** connecting a rope to another object such as a carabiner, sling, or another rope.
- **Bight:** refers to the entire length or section of rope between the ends.
- **Working end:** is the rope part used during knot-tying.
- **Standing end:** the unused portion of the rope during knot tying.

There are at least a hundred kinds of different knots, bends, and hitches out there. However, the only ones you need to know are the ones that are useful for mountaineers and climbers. Learning these enables you to accomplish most climbing tasks such as rappelling, building anchors, and securing ropes to a harness or carabiner.

We have here the following six essential climbing knots, hitches, and bends that will allow you to complete many fundamental climbing tasks - from securing the rope to a harness to rappelling and building anchors.

- Autoblock Knot
- Clove Hitch
- Double Fisherman's
- Figure 8 Follow Through Knot (Rewoven Figure 8 Knot)
- Girth Hitch
- Overhand Bend (European Death Knot)

Climbing Knots, Hitches, and Bends

Mastering climbing knots is a crucial skill for every rock or mountain climber and must be among the fundamental knowledge you must learn if you aspire to be a rock climber. There are several rock climbing knots, and all have their purpose that can be useful to your climbing endeavor.

Since you will be working with ropes extensively when rock climbing, mountaineering, and rappelling, learning how to tie knots properly can be lifesaving in critical situations. Understanding and using the right climbing knot for each position can save you from falling and avoiding severe accidents. Acquiring this skill is worth investing your time and effort in. Not only that, learning knot tying may come in handy in your day-to-day life - that is, from hanging hammocks, making fish nets, and macrame projects like bags, belts, and planters.

As you gain more experience in rock climbing, the more you will learn about knots, but knowing a few will give you the edge over other newbie climbers. For the most part, climbing knots are pretty easy to make, and you can learn some of them very quickly. Nonetheless, it would be best if you practiced a lot to master the art of knot tying, mainly when your life depends on it when you're up on the mountain. When this happens, you will be thankful for the time you spent learning.

Six Essential Knots, Glitches, and Bends

Many knots are helpful for climbing but learning the following six essential climbing knots, hitches, and bends allow you to complete many fundamental climbing tasks - from securing the rope to a harness to rappelling and building anchors.

Autoblock Knot

Rappelling can be a dangerous aspect of rock climbing, for you have to rely on equipment, anchors, and climbing buddy. Therefore, it is vital to take proper precautions to minimize the risks of rappelling. It is where an autoblock becomes handy. You use the autoblock knot for safety backup.

The autoblock knot lets you:

- Stop and safely hang while clearing rope snags

- Free twists and knots from the rope
- Toss the rope farther down the cliff
- It keeps you from losing control
- It will stop you if you get hit by a falling rock

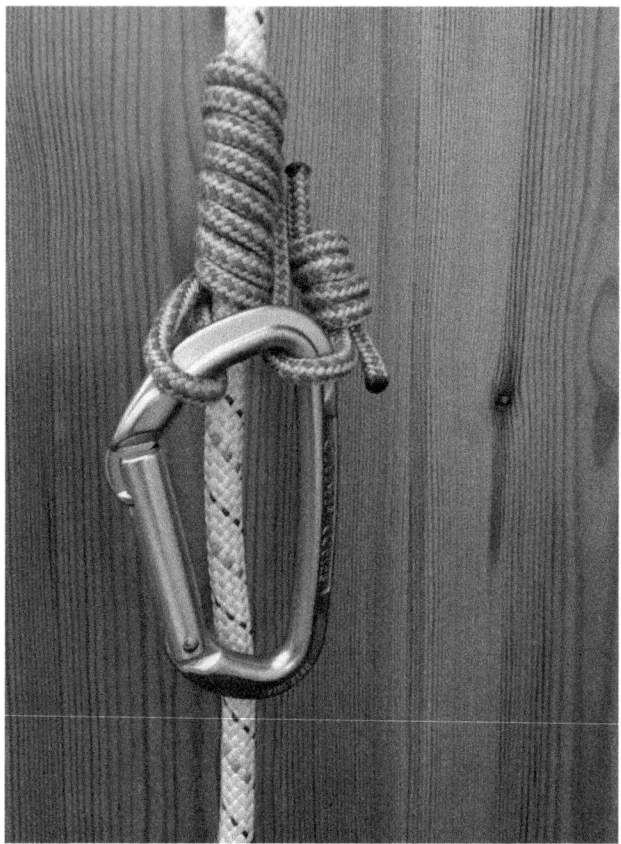

Furthermore, the autoblock knot allows you to rappel slowly and stay in control. It is useful, especially on free and overhanging rappels when you can't touch the rock.

Here's how to do the autoblock knot.

1. Clip a locking carabiner onto the loop of your harness on the sides where your brake hand will be.
2. Wrap the autoblock cord 4-5 times around the rappel ropes.

3. On your harness leg loop, clip both ends of the cord into the locking carabiner. Be sure that it is not tight, so it easily slides as you rappel.

Clove Hitch

The Clove Hitch is another easy-to-do tying technique, which is famous because of its versatility. Aside from giving the climbers a secure knot, they can easily lengthen or shorten it anytime without untying or retying. Once connected to the anchor point in the rock wall, climbers need to feed an extra rope length at either side of the hitch to get them closer or farther from the anchor, making shifting positions as easy and secure as possible.

On the other hand, if you're suspended and want to connect to an anchor, you can grab the rope in your fist with your finger, making a loop. Next, bring your hand up and clip the cord into the carabiner. Repeat this to make another loop. Finish the hitch by pulling the resulting strands tightly.

The clove hitch is pretty easy to untie after taking a heavy load and quickly detaches itself as you unclip it from the carabiner, allowing mountaineers to secure their rope on a carabiner. You can even do this with one hand, so many climbers use this to connect directly to an anchor while climbing as well. To do this, you must first hold the rope and form a loop by crossing the rope over itself once. Next, create the second loop by repeating the previous step, moving it behind the first loop, and collating both loops with a carabiner.

When you happen to be at the anchor, you may likewise tie the clove while holding into the anchor carabiner with one hand. Grab the rope in your fist and a finger pointing down, then bring your hand up so that your finger points up and toward you. Clip the rope into the carabiner. Grab the rope below the carabiner and repeat the same. Grab it with your finger pointing down, and then bring it up so that your finger points up and toward you. Clip it to the carabines and pull both strands up to dress the hitch.

Double Fisherman's Knot (Grapevine Knot)

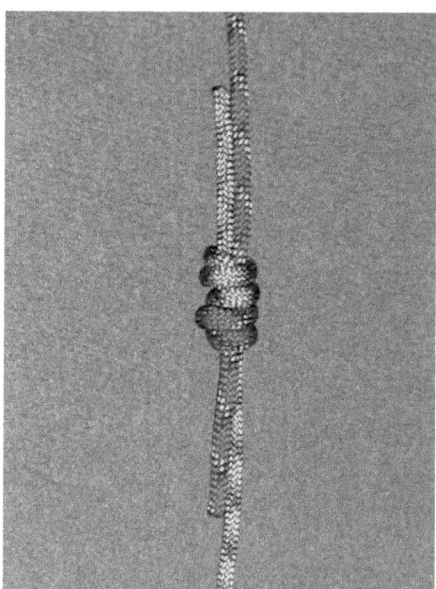

Every climber or mountaineer knows that the ropes available for sale have a fixed length standard. So whenever they need an extra length, they have to provide another rope and attach the two. Many knots can be used to tie ropes together securely but, being one of the easiest, the Double Fisherman's Knot is the most popular. The reason behind this is that the knot creates two stoppers that prevent the rope from slipping or detaching when being used.

One secure way of joining together two ropes is by using the Double Fisherman's knot.

To make a Double Fisherman's Knot:

- Bring two ends of the rope together, allowing them to overlap.
- With your thumb over the rope, hold the end of one rope in your fist.
- Tie the working end of the rope over your thumb and the first rope, bringing it under and wrapping it again to form an "X."
- Slide your thumb out and feed the rope through the "X." Pull the knot tight.
- Pull the other rope and repeat it. The rope that you just pulled through is now the new working end.
- Form an X on your thumb with the rope and push the working end through it. Now you have two knots with two strands of ropes in between,
- Pull them tight to dress the knots, and then pull the outer ropes to bring the knots together.

The completed Double Fisherman's Knot should have two Xs and four parallel strands on the other side. Ensure that both ropes have about 18 inches left for the tail for tying two ropes together for rappelling. About three inches of the tail is required when making loops with an accessory cord.

Figure 8 Follow Through

An essential type of all climbing knots, the figure of eight follow-through is used to tie a rope into the climber's harness to provide a high friction link to their most important gear. It can also be connected to a bight or a rope bend, allowing the climber to create a strong loop fixed on an anchor.

Girth Hitch

One easy way to connect a loop of webbing or cord to your harness's tie-points is through a Girth Hitch. To do the hitch, circle one end of the loop around a carabiner (or any object) and feed the other end through the first loop before pulling it snug tight.

Overhand Bend

Well-known to mountaineers as the European death knot, the overhand bend is used to join two rappelling ropes effectively. The key benefit is that it ensures that you won't get stuck on the wall while pulling down the ropes since the knot flattens out once loaded. To do this, join the two ropes together and tie an overhand knot using both strands. The ropes should run entirely parallel throughout the knot. Next, pull all four strands tightly to dress and tighten the resulting knot.

Other Climbing Knots, Hitches, and Bends

Although not considered essential, the following knots, hitches, and bends are commonly used in climbing, especially for intermediate and advanced techniques.

Bowline Knot

The bowline is similar to Sheet Bend in structure. In both knots, bight locks into a loop. However, a bowline knot uses the bight while using the loop in the sheet bend is usual.

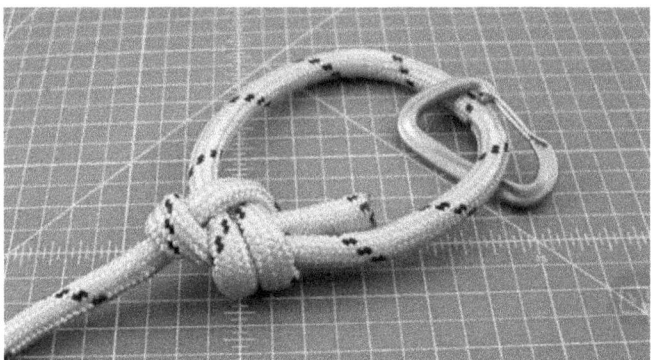

Double Bowline Knot

The Double Bowline, also known as *Round-Turn Bowline*, is a classic bowline knot with a pair of overhand loops or a supplementary wrapping turn around the bight. This extra strength and durability make the Double Bowline suitable for arduous activities and intense rigging. Another benefit of this knot is that it is easier to unfasten after being weighted in a fall. For such a reason, it has become a favorite knot by sport climbers who usually take multiple lead falls.

To do the Double Bowline knot, you have to:

1. Place the rope across your left hand, leaving the free end dangling.
2. Create two small loops by wrapping the line on hand around your thumb twice, then laying them on your palm.
3. Get the free end and insert it through the two loops from the underside.
4. Next, wrap the line around the standing line and down through the pair of loops.
5. Pull the free end while holding the vertical line to secure the knot.

Barrel Knot

The Barrel Knot is a slip or friction knot since it automatically tightens around the object (e.g., a parachute cord or leather) it is tied to when weighted. Sometimes, though incorrectly, this knot is also called the Blood knot. This knot is an excellent option for closing a belay system and  stopping the rope's end from unexpectedly feeding through the belay device.

Making a Barrel Knot is pretty straightforward. Firstly, you have to make a loop with the end of the rope. Make another loop and insert the end into the loops. To finish, pull both ends.

Bowline on a Bight

A bowline on a bight is a bowline that is formed with just one rope. This knot is perfect to create a dependable loop, but both line ends are unavailable. Many consider it a better knot than the Figure 8 Knot because of its ability to quickly untie after a severe fall when tied to a climbing harness. Nevertheless, this knot can be reinforced with solid support knots with long tail-ends.

To make a bowline on a bight Knot, you have to:

1. First, form a loop by passing the end of the bight over the part of a vertical line.
2. Pull the end through the loop to form the knot.
3. Open the bright and bring it around the whole knot, pulling it up until it surrounds the standing ends.
4. Hold and secure the standing part, then pull the loop down to strengthen the knot.

Buntline Hitch

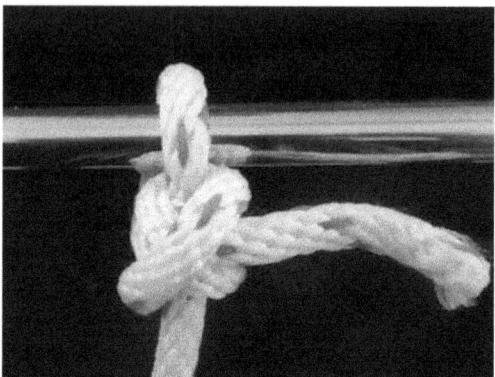

The Buntline Hitch was initially used in securing the bottom edge of a sail in square-rigged ships to the buntline. The continual yanking and shaking during the sail makes the knot further reinforce it. This type of knot functions well in today's slick synthetic ropes.

Unfortunately, you cannot tie Buntline Hitch under a load. The presence of a heavy load means the rope is pulled down; thus, the knot will be more difficult to release.

Here's what you need to do to form a Buntline Hitch:

- Run the rope end around the support.
- Wrap it around the standing line, ultimately making an "8" figure.
- Run the end through the loop you just formed.
- Hold the end part and pull to secure the knot, and you're done.

Figure 8 Bend

The Figure 8 Bend, also referred to as the *Flemish Bend*, is a double "8" loop. It connects two ropes of similar diameters. This knot is often described as an easy-to-remember and secure knot and can be quickly untied even under high strain. For obvious security reasons, don't use figure 8 bend in ropes that hugely differ in diameter.

1. For an "8" loop with the first rope, trace the first loop with the second rope to create the twin loop.
2. Pull both ends of the two loops to tighten the knot. You can also cut tag ends to keep them roughly 3 to 4 inches long.

Figure on Eight Bight

When it comes to Figure 8 on a Bight Knot, you need to double the rope into a bight then create the figure "8" knot. It is one of the best methods in making a figure "8" loop other than the Figure 8 Follow Through style. The flexible knot assists in linking a rope to a climbing harness or carabiner.

To make this knot, create a loop using the bight of a rope, then run the end through the loop. You can finalize it by pulling both ends to tighten the knot.

Fisherman's Knot

Fisherman's Knot, also called the *English Knot*, includes two overhand knots. Each of these knots is tied around the standing part of each other's line. Even if the Fisherman's Knot is typically utilized as a bend to link two lines, it can also be used to tie the ends of a single length of rope to create a loop.

The advantages of this knot type lie in its symmetry, strength, and sturdiness. Even climbers who have cold, wet hands can execute this tie.

1. Create a loop with one rope over a second rope, and then run its end through the loop.
2. Form another loop with the second rope, and then tuck its end into the said loop.
3. Tighten both knots by their tag ends to secure.
4. Pull the standing lines to tighten both knots close together.

Munter Hitch

It is only natural for gear to get broken after using them for a time, and mountaineering gear isn't an exception. A Munter hitch can be done whenever the climber's belay device gets damaged, preventing the climber from wasting time during the climb because of it. The Munter hitch works just like a belay device; it slows the climber down during the descent, making abseiling or rappelling as safe as possible.

Munter Mule

The Munter Mule is a mixture of both the Munter and Mule Hitches. This knot is specially designed for both canyoneering and rock climbing. It enables climbers to go hands-free during belay and can be untied even under tension.

1. Entwine the rope end twice through the carabiner.
2. Take the end part up and run it to the right side.
3. Form two loops with the end part of the rope.
4. Run the right loop through the left one, and then bring that loop back to the ride side.

5. Finalize the knot by running the right loop over the standing line and tucking it to the loop formed through that crossover; pull to secure.

Overhand Bend

Well-known to mountaineers as the European death knot, the overhand bend is used to join two rappelling ropes effectively. The key benefit is that it ensures that you won't get stuck on the wall while pulling down the ropes since the knot flattens out once loaded. To do this, join the two ropes together and tie an overhand knot using both strands. The ropes should run entirely parallel throughout the knot. Next, pull all four strands tightly to dress and tighten the resulting knot.

Overhand Knot

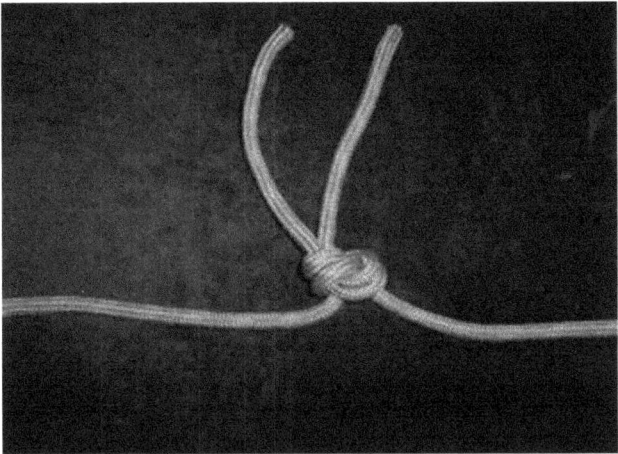

The Overhand Knot is a basic knot commonly used almost everywhere. It is the first single-strand knot we learn as kids.

Forming the Overhand Knot is quite simple—Run the tag end over the standing part of the line. Tuck the line end inside the loop and pull it out. Pull both ends to secure the knot.

Prusik Climbing Knot

Also known as third hands or autoblocks, learning the prusik knot is essential yet straightforward knowledge to every climber. The prusik's purpose is to attach a carabiner to the climber's harness by using an accessory cord and grabbing the rope, stopping you from traveling downwards whenever weight has been put on it. In other words, it simply serves as the climber's 'third hand' that holds the rope in place while they are busy using their own hands in other things such as holding on to rocks or putting anchors in place.

Commonly used to support rappels, the autoblock is easy to do.

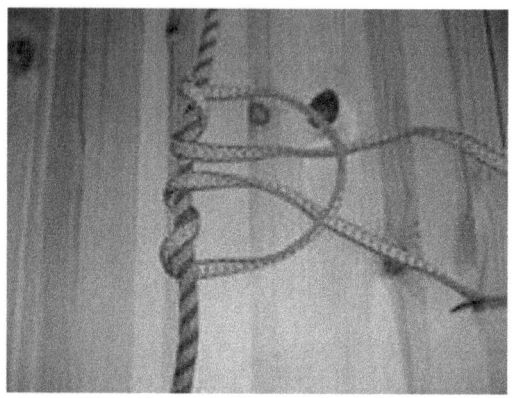

First, place your loop behind the two ropes, resulting in a large loop in one rope and a small loop to another. Tie a joining knot on the smaller loop close to the ropes and slightly offset to prevent it from going to the bend of the resulting loop. Next, wrap the large loop around the ropes until there are only two small loops left and clip it to the carabiner. Make sure that the loops run parallel towards one another while gripping the rope at the same time.

Stopper Knot

Usually tied to the bottom or end of the rope, a stopper knot stops the climber from slipping to the end of their ropes by proving an obstacle hard to pass through. It prevents you from dying or getting injured whenever your abseiling or rappelling fails, which is a common mistake in both rock climbing and mountaineering. Mountaineers also use this knot to straighten extra lengths of rope left over after making a figure of eights for their harnesses, not only keeping them from getting tangled but also adding up to another layer of security.

Tensionless Hitch

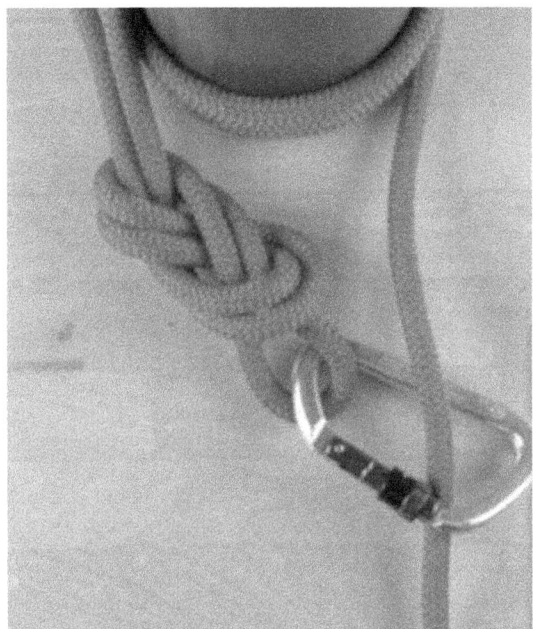

The Tensionless Hitch is designed to carry a hefty load, that is, you as the climber. The knot does not cause considerable stress on the rope. The rope's anchor, whose diameter should be at least eight times that of the rope, must be sturdy enough to withstand the rotational forces applied on the knot.

1. Wind the rope at least four times around the anchor.
2. Create a bight using the shorter end of the line.
3. For a Figure "8" knot with it and pull both ends to secure.
4. Secure the knot by clipping it and the standing line with a carabiner.

Trucker's Hitch

The Trucker's Hitch is a great knot to fasten a load firmly. It is a combination of knots that allows a rope to be pulled quite tight, just like a guitar string. The knot obtained its name from the truckers since they have used it to secure heavy loads in place.

To make a Trucker's Hitch:

1. Form a slippery half hitch at the center of the rope.
2. Run the end line through a bar or cleat and bring it up to the loop.

3.   Pass the end through the loop and pull it tight.

4.   Secure the loop by making 1 to 2 half hitches around one or both lines.

Water Knot

The Water Knot is also known as the Overhand Follow Through, Ring Bend, Tape Knot, and Grass Knot. You can link flat materials such as leather or tape with this knot. It is a strong knot that can bear a lot of pressure on the condition that the tail ends are of sufficient length.

1.   Make a loop with the first rope, running the end through it.
2.   to tighten halfway through, and then run the second rope through the knot.
3.   Run the end of the second rope to the back, crossing through the frontal wrap of the first knot.
4.   Secure both ends by pulling them away, and you're done.

Yosemite Bowline

A variation of Bowline Knot, the Yosemite Bowline has its free end entwined around one side of the loop and secured back into a knot. This method boosts the strength of the knot and stops it from inverting to the perilous Slip Knot.

1.   Create a small loop by the end of the rope and run the tag end through that loop.

2. Run the end behind the standing part of the line, passing it out through the loop.

3. Run it through the big loop, then back up through the small loop.

4. To secure, hold and pull the standing line before doing the same to the end line.

Zeppelin Bend Knot

The Zeppelin Bend Knot, sometimes called the Rosendahl Bend Knot, ties two ropes together. Aside from being an easy knot to connect, it is also very secure and jam-proof.

To do it:

1. Start forming a "6" with one rope - the running line on the underside and create figure "9" with the other rope with the running line over. Lay figure 6 partially on top of the rope formed as a figure "9".

2. Take the rope's end that forms figure "6" and pass it through the opening rope, creating figure "9" and figure "6".

3. Repeat it with the end of the rope with "9" in the opposite direction via the opening of the rope, forming **"6" before passing through the opening of the** rope forming "9." Pull ends tight to form the Zeppelin Bend Knot.

4. Take the end of "6" and pass it through the opening of "9" and "6".

5. Repeat with the end of "9" in the opposite direction - through the opening of "6" and the opening of "6".

6. Pull ends tight.

Climbing Anchors

Whether you're lead climbing or top-rope climbing, learning how to build a solid anchor is critical to your safety as a climber.

A climbing anchor consists of pieces of climbing gears set up to support the weight of a climber or belayer. It is an essential component of sport climbing, leading traditional routes, top-roping, rappelling, and multi-pitch belay stations.

While specific anchor building requirements differ from climb to climb, all styles of rope climbing share the same basic principles. The acronym SERENE summarizes these simple yet effective guidelines.

S—Solid

Each piece of the anchor requires solidity to the greatest possible extent. While you can't expect all components of the climbing anchor to withstand high loads, each must achieve the most robust placements possible. To distinguish between an adequately strong and an average solid point in a climbing anchor, you may refer to an AMGA-certified guide for help.

E—Equalized

While it is impossible to build an anchor with all its parts withstanding high loads, creating one with a load distributed to its components can decrease the chance of breakage of any of its features.

R—Redundant

All anchor system components require a backup so that a single point of failure won't result in a catastrophic failure of the whole anchor system. If a failure occurs in one protection point or any point in the anchor system is cut, another layer of protection must take the load. The usual practice is using two bolts at the top of a sport climb and three or more pieces of active or passive trad gear at the top of a trad climb.

E—Efficient

Efficiency in an anchor system refers to an attempt to find a timely and straightforward solution to the issue at hand. Keeping things simple yet efficient can save time and, therefore, easier to evaluate the whole system. If every anchor takes 5 minutes to build on a long route, it means a longer time to your climbing hours.

NE—No Extension

The design of the anchor system must eliminate shock-loading of the remaining components in case one component fails. Any slackness in the system resulting from a failing member component will direct an enormous load on other parts or components.

How to Build Rock Climbing Anchors

A climbing anchor consists of interconnecting anchor points, including a master point where the rope and climbers are clipped and securely attached to the rock. It would be best to consider many factors when building an anchor. However, the process goes down to two basic steps.

It would be best to consider many factors when building an anchor. However, the process goes down to two basic steps.

- Identifying and creating the anchor points to be used as part of the whole system
- Connecting anchor points by utilizing any of the several techniques.

Step #1 - Identifying Anchor Points

The first step to building an anchor is to identify what you will be using as anchor points. Your choice depends mainly on where you are and the available gear.

Natural Anchors

Natural elements like trees and boulders are natural anchors that are good and can help you conserve other gear. However, you need to assess their integrity correctly to ensure safety. Let's examine them closely.

Trees

Before selecting a tree for anchor, make sure that it is alive, solid, and well-rooted. You can't easily trust a tree that's growing out of cliffs, so always test a tree by pushing it with a foot.

As a rule of thumb, choose a healthy tree that is at least 12 inches in diameter.

When using a tree as an anchor, encircle its base with a runner and clip the ends together with a carabiner, or you may girth-hitch a long runner around it.

Rock Features

Examples of rock features you can utilize as anchors are horns and chockstones – a stone that's tightly wedged in a crack. To check on the integrity of these rock features, make sure that they are solid and well-attached. Search for brittle rock and cracks that indicate a weakness.

You can loop as a runner over the top of horns and clip it to the rope. As for chockstones, encircle it with a runner and clip ends together with a carabiner or girth-hitch the runner.

Fixed Anchors

Any artificial gear that serves as a permanent fixture to the rock is called a fixed anchor. You have to clip quickdraws or runners to the equipment to attach the rope. Common examples of fixed anchors are pitons and bolts.

Like natural anchors, you have to check fixed anchors for signs of weakness thoroughly. It is not trustworthy if there are signs of cracks, wear, or excessive corrosion.

Also, don't use it as an anchor if the bolt or piston moves in any direction. Avoid using out-of-date gear, especially 1/4-inch bolts and sheet-metal style hangers. Instead, use the standard bolt size, which is 3/8 to 1/2 inches in diameter.

Step #2 - Connecting the Anchor Points

In building the anchor, you have to connect the individual anchor points to create a master point.

A standard one will consist of two to three anchor points that hold downward pull and keep an upward pull.

You must connect these anchor points and balance them to distribute the load equally. You can balance the anchor by using runners or a long section of accessory cord. We call this cord a cordelette.

Methods of Equalizing an Anchor

There are two basic methods of equalizing the anchor.

- Static Equalization
- Self-Equalization

Static Equalization

Static Equalization refers to an anchor system with multiple anchor points tied together. An anchor system that is tied off has no slack or adjustability feature, and they are perfect for climbs with a clear direction of pull, such as straight down.

So, if you anticipate the direction of pull changing, better build a self-equalizing anchor.

To create static Equalization, using a cordelette anchor is the popular way of connecting two, three, or more anchor points.

In making a cordelette, utilize an 18-20 ft. long section of a seven to eight-millimeter Perlon accessory cord. Use a double fisherman's loop to tie a cord into one big circle.

How to Equalize a Three-Anchor Points with a Cordelette

1. First, clip the cordelette into each piece with a carabiner, then pull down the top sections between the components.

2. Connect sections with the lower part of the cordelette by bringing them together and clip a locking carabiner to all three loops.

3. Then pull down the carabiner to distribute equally the tension in all strands of the cordelette.

4. The fisherman's knot must be positioned below the highest anchor point to clear out the master point knot that you will be tying.

5. Determine the source of the force on the anchor and pull the carabiner towards that direction.

6. Using the figure-eight knot, tie all sections together to create the master point. Alternatively, if you don't have enough rope to tie a figure eight, tie an overhand knot. These two knots are both practical, although the overhand is much more challenging to untie after it has been weighted,

To make sure that all three anchor points are equally weighted, give the carabiner a tug.

The primary attachment to the anchor is the master point, which the loop is created by tying figure eight. It is where you and your belayer will clip in. One drawback of the cordelette is when there is a change in the direction of the pull; one piece in the anchor syIn self-equalization, the design of the anchor system allows adjustments changes in the direction of pull to distribute the load equally to all anchor points. If you are aware that the direction of the pull will change throughout the climb, choose to create a self-equalizing anchor.

A great option at the loop of a sport climb where you have two side-by-side bolts is an anchor. In making a quad anchor, follow the following steps:stem will be taking the entire load.

Self-Equalization

In self-equalization, the design of the anchor system allows adjustments changes in the direction of pull to distribute the load equally to all anchor points. If you are aware that the direction of the pull will change throughout the climb, choose to create a self-equalizing anchor.

A great option at the loop of a sport climb where you have two side-by-side bolts is an anchor. In making a quad anchor, follow the following steps:

1. Get your cordelette and fold it to have four equal-length strands.

2. In the ends of both strands nearest to the double fisherman's bend, clip a locking carabiner.

3. Clip that carabiner into one of the bolts
4. You hold the opposite end of the cordelette loop up to the other bolt.
5. Take the low point in your cordelette and loop it around your fist. On either side of your fist, tie an overhand knot, about eight apart.
6. Clip both strands of the free ends of your cordelette loop with a g carabiner and clip that same carabiner into the remaining bolt.

By clipping two opposing locking carabiners into three of the strands that run between the knots, you tied earlier, build the powerpoint of your anchor. It is where the top rope will clip in. However, leave the fourth strand free. It will limit the carabiner in case that one side of the anchor fails to function correctly.

A relatively straightforward way of connecting two anchor points while creating m that adjusts to the direction of the pull is what we call the sliding X.

To create the sliding X, you have to clip a single sling to the carabiner at each anchor point. Then grab the top part of the sling and make a half twist before clipping a locking carabiner into the twist and around the lower part of the sling.

One drawback though of the sliding X is that, if one point fails, a significant extension will shock load the other anchor point.

Another way to construct a self-equalizing anchor is through an equalette by combining elements from the sliding X and the cordelette. This way, it provides effective self-equalization and easy adjustability. Climbers often used an equalette on multiple trad climbing.

Follow these steps to make an equalette:

Climbing Techniques

Strength is essential in rock climbing, but it is the climbing technique that makes great climbers.

Using the correct technique can make the climb more accessible, and as you start climbing with the right moves and procedures, the climb that looks impossible at the start will soon give you clues.

Climbing techniques include correct use of feet and hands, maintaining balance, and efficient ways to climb. To perform such actions and methods, you need to master balance, footwork, handwork, grips, and deliberate moves.

If you're on your way to mastering rock climbing, let's learn some basic and advanced techniques in climbing.

Footwork

In rock climbing, your limbs present a solid point for support, and climbers tend to rely on their feet. Reliance on the feet, especially beginners, makes foot techniques one of the essential rock climbing moves and techniques.

Footwork techniques require great precision and must therefore have to be carried out with coordination. It's best to perfect your footwork on more accessible routes to avoid accidents.

Edging

Edging is considered essential footwork as it is basic to rock and sport climbing. Climbers use this technique every time they have to climb.

While climbing, you will come across footholds that are small enough to fit your shoes. To support your body weight, you have to place the tip of your toe or the internal/external edge of your climbing shoe.

You perform edging using the inside edge of your climbing shoe. If you are moving sideways along the rock surface or wall, the outside edging comes into play. When edging, you have to push your body while searching for the next handhold to provide your body with balance and stability as you plan your next move.

Smearing

The crucial element in smearing is the contact made by the rubber to the rock, which is the best attachment to sloping holds. For those where the foot tends to slip, exert more pressure to ensure attachment. It's best to practice smearing on bouldering routes with bug handholds and slightly inclined smooth boulders.

As you move upward, you will not get footholds for every step. Sometimes, there will only be rock slabs or vertical walls that provide no support to your feet. It is when the smearing technique becomes handy.

When smearing, you will press your climbing shoe directly to the surface of the wall or rock to gain the friction for your upward moves. By applying pressure on your toes, your waist and body are pushed out of the wall. To do this, you have to be more creative, flexible and have a natural sense of balance. With the proper smearing technique, you can quickly move upward through the steep and vertical terrains.

You may carry out smearing on different footholds, unlike edging. Instead of relying on weight, smearing depends mainly on friction. Pressure is exerted on the holds by employing the toes and footballs.

Flagging

Another essential technique you can use for smooth climbing is flagging. It allows a climber to counterbalance the body with the free-hanging foot evenly while balancing your body weight. This technique is to avoid swinging out from the rock and to move higher.

There are two kinds of flags - the **rear flags** and the **side flags.**

The rear flag is when you place the free leg behind nearly 90 degrees to your standing leg. Climbers would use rear flagging when moving to the opposite direction of their firmly holding foot and hand. In the side flag, climbers would flag one foot straight while pushing the foothold with their other foot.

Stemming

When climbers come across corners and dihedrals of rocky walls, they use the stemming technique to push one foot on one wall and another foot on the other wall. This technique is applicable even on smooth surfaces where there are no footholds, cracks, or jugs.

When stemming, you rely heavily on the strength of your feet against the walls. Counter pressure is an essential basis for exerting pressure, and stemming involves exerting pressure on two opposing surfaces. This efficient technique is carried out with the hands or feet and is best carried out with the leg muscles.

Because there is nothing to hold to push you up, you need your force to do it by pushing the wall with your hands and feet so that you can move upward. Once you encounter footholds or jugs while stemming, your climb can become much more manageable.

Bat-Hang

Here is one underrated technique in climbing—the bat-hang. Only a few high-ranking climbers can perform this move. You hang upside down from the wall like a bat, using only your toes, as the name implies.

There must be a steep wall with a hole large enough to accommodate both feet to do the bat-hang technique. Position the edge of the hold right above your toe joints and position your legs perpendicularly with your toes and feet. They must be straight and tense.

Climbers would use the bat-hang to rest their arms, and when they are in a position where they must climb through a jug with feet first before grabbing the next hold with their hand.

Lay-Backing

Laybacks are best carried out when there are available strong footholds for support. It is performed by pulling a part of the crack using your hands while pushing your feet against the other side. When there's not enough room to allow lay-backing, use smearing instead.

Hooking

Hooking is an easy technique that you can carry out using your toes and heels. You can perform the hooking process by placing the toe on the hold and pulling the body's weight upward. It is often used in overhanging routes and keeping close to the wall or rock surface.

The heel hooking technique is performed by placing the foot on holds and often above the body or at the same level of the body before pushing the body's weight upwards. It is the most commonly used hooking technique and can be performed naturally even without practice. However, it's still best to be familiar with the method.

Jugs

Jugs are often the first handholds encountered by climbers, which are very easy to complete as they are large and have enough space for gripping. Climbers would grip jugs from hanging positions to push their body weight. Remember not to grab jugs from chest level.

When exerting too much pressure in gripping jugs, it can quickly tire you. Jugs provide the right spots for re-chalking, brief rests, adjusting, and changing gear.

Crimpers

Crimps are those edges small enough for a finger to wrap around. Crimping is done by placing your finger around the tiny edge, curling the fingers, and covering the thumb over the index finger. Observe caution when trying to carry out crimping as it exerts stress on fingers. It can easily result in injuries. You may try to practice crimping on a fingerboard.

Pockets

Natural and artificial climbing routes have several holds. You may apply the pocket technique by placing your finger into these small holds and wrapping it around them.

Pocket is a bit similar to crimping as pockets give more room for gripping. However, before gripping, check for more space in the holds and observe caution.

Pinches

The pinch technique likewise relies mainly on the thumb, but like in the crimping procedure, it does not require climbers to curl a finger around the holds. Instead, they should wrap them around the olds and use their thumb to pinch deep into the holds.

Slopers

Slopers are big, round, and inclined holds that a climber can easily find in a natural setting. It requires precision along with careful distribution of body weight.

Friction is significant to sloping that best climbers had to chalk well before performing this technique.

In sloping, climbers would place their forehands on the holds with forearms straight, and fingers close together for more strength.

Underclings and Side Pull

Both undercling and side pull techniques are position-dependent. Raise the feet high towards the waist and push your body upwards with arms straight to perform underlings.

Side pulls work the same but in a different position. Doing side pulls can be a bit tricky as they are carried out by pulling sideways.

Manteling

Manteling moves are done on wide ledges and are performed using the hands to press down the hold. Providing the basis for support are the shoulder muscles.

Rock-Over

Rock-over is one of the basic climbing techniques which involve transferring your weight from one foot to the other. You must be aware of the center of gravity that's usually at its strongest around your belly button. The secret is to quickly transfer your weight from one foot to the other and hit the next point of balance before moving forward.

Chapter 5: Training to Climb

Getting ready for your first mountaineering journey requires acquiring the necessary technical skills. Unless you are physically and mentally prepared for the challenges that await you, you surely won't make it to the summit. If a professional guide leads your mountaineering activity, the itinerary is likely to include a few days to learn essential snow and ice skills. However, the necessary physical training will take weeks or months to prepare.

As you can see, training is an essential component of any rock climbing or mountaineering.

Mountaineering fitness requires a high overall level of physical conditioning. While you need to climb at varying degrees of intensity and navigate challenging terrains, you need to improve cardiovascular and motor fitness. The greater levels of fitness, the more you can efficiently adjust to altitude or acclimatize.

By developing cardiovascular fitness, e.g., the fitness of the heart and lungs and motor fitness, particularly strength, endurance, balance, and strength, the more you can efficiently achieve your goal of reaching the summit.

Goal Setting

Your training needs will depend on the type of mountaineering you will be undergoing - whether expedition-style or alpine-style. The most common is alpine mountaineering which involves a straightforward climb that doesn't require high-altitude porters and supplemental oxygen. Conversely, expedition climbs have a fixed line of stocked camps along the route and involve expedition staff to travel up and down the route to set up camps and fix ropes.

Both styles, however, will require training and within both categories are a range of routes with different difficulty ratings.

Your goals should suit your lifestyle and must be constructed in a way that will develop and maintain your strength, power, endurance, flexibility, and technique. More importantly, it should be designed to motivate you into training regularly. It should also help you lessen the chances of injury and maximize your recovery during intervals.

You have to ensure that the training varies so that you can handle different situations during the climb. For instance, training on the same wall every day will not improve your ability to climb different crags. Make routines and setting variations one of your top priorities.

Another variable to consider is your training target. Would it be for the long, medium, or short term? Long-term means this season or the next; medium-term can be within the next three months; and short-term can be today or within two to three weeks. While most climbers prefer to climb during summer, you should consider having short, medium, and long-term goals.

Identifying your limitations and weaknesses is also a huge help. A small improvement in those "weaknesses" can have a drastic change in the effect of your performance. Likewise, a slight deterioration in those weaknesses can also have enormous adverse effects. Thus, allocating more time to work on those weaknesses will generate more benefits later on.

A helpful mnemonic can help you focus on setting your goals—SMARTER. It means:

- **Specific**: You want to climb where? What peak do you want to reach?
- **Measurable**: Use numbers and grades to help you determine what you want of your goal.
- **Achievable**: Can you achieve your goal within the specified target time with your current abilities and skills?
- **Realistic**: Is your goal workable? You might have set it too high that may result in failure and frustration.
- **Timely**: You need to set a deadline on your goal, or you might fall into the temptation of procrastination.
- **Exciting**: Your goal must inspire and motivate you to work on it.
- **Re-evaluated and Reviewed**: Record your goal and keep track of your training so that you can monitor both regularly. It also helps to have someone know about your goal and help remind you to keep working to achieve it.

To achieve a climb that is slightly beyond your current fitness level, you need to ensure that your training plan will push you further beyond what you are capable of doing before.

You must customize your approach according to your need and the particular mountain you're attempting to climb for your training plan. So, here are the general steps to follow when making plans for your mountaineering.

Assess Your Fitness Level

You may need an evaluation by a certified trainer. If you go with a reputable guide service, they will appropriately orient you on the physical preparedness and requirements, including medical history.

Consider the Physical Requirements

Climbing a mountain essentially involves endurance. You assess your needs carefully and plan accordingly based on the particular climb you're planning to undergo. The key objective of your training plan is to climb at a steady rate without stopping and having enough energy and strength to descend safely.

Design Your Training Plan

Mountaineering requires multiple types of training which focus on different needs.

- **Cardio workouts—** for the improvement of the overall fitness level of lungs and heart.
- **Interval sessions boost** your ability to maximize the amount of oxygen intake and process it for optimal use.
- **Strength and Endurance Exercises—**for sustaining physical output needed for long hours while hauling a heavy load.
- **Hiking Days—**for extending your training into real-life situations

Preparation means a lot when it comes to rock climbing. It demands a higher level of fitness and experience to ascend a wide variety of terrains. Having said this, you have to focus on training and enhancing both your mind and body for the endurance ahead. To top it all, you will also need to be equipped to work against gravity, pushing your whole body at high altitudes.

Anybody can do rock climbing as long as they are healthy, determined, and well-prepared. Whether you choose bouldering or trad climbing, training is always essential before heading to the actual challenge.

"Train, train, train!" should be the mantra of any rock climber, but before immersing yourself in full-blown training, you have to lay out a comprehensive plan. Your training program has to be customized for you and the project you will undertake. To give you a general idea, below are the four essential points a climber has to observe for their training plan:

Gauging Your Present Fitness Level & Physical Prerequisites of Your Climb

Rock climbing demands a certain level of fitness, which is why a physical evaluation from your physician and a certified trainer is a must. In some cases, a reputable guide service will ask you to submit a complete medical history.

Moreover, rock climbing is a strength and endurance event, with some disciplines requiring you to carry a substantial load while ascending steep terrain up to a high altitude. That being said, you must determine your needs attentively and plan accordingly.

To grasp the general idea if your present condition applies to the requirements of your target project, ask yourself these questions:

What is the current state of my physical health?

1.   What are the strengths and weaknesses of my current motor fitness?
2.   What are my present cardiovascular strengths and weaknesses?

What is the required fitness on the climb?

1.   What type of climbing and terrain will I need to do?
2.   How many days does the climb demand?
3.   How high is the climb?
4.   How heavy is the load I must carry during the climb?

How long will it take for me to train in order to pass the requirement of the climb?

Deciding on Your Training Approach

Your plan doesn't need to be something expensive. It can be made personally with a minimal budget, and all you need to do is conduct proper research. If you have friends who are already experts, don't hesitate to ask their opinion about it. Conversely, if you had the budget, it would be much better to seek out the help of a personal trainer in coming up with a customized plan with regular check-ins. This way, you will gain expert feedback and someone to keep your motivation up. Furthermore, you will enjoy a broad scope of training options.

Developing a Customized Training Plan

Rock climbing necessitates several types of training, with each particular paying attention to:

- Cardiovascular exercises: for general fitness
- Interval sessions: for improving your ability to manage your oxygen intake
- Strength and endurance workouts: for keeping up physical output for longer hours
- Flexibility and balance training: for your body to adapt and carry out the necessary moves during the feat
- Hiking: for more practice and experience in outdoor terrains

Warming Up

The idea of warming up can be so dull that you might end up skipping it. However, getting your body ready for the project is a crucial step. Warming up and stretching prevents injuries like swollen forearms or finger injuries. On the other hand, overdoing a warm-up may lead to over fatigue. It is advisable to take a breather for about 30 to 45 seconds at the end of each exercise unless noted otherwise.

With these points in mind, one must have a customized warm-up ritual. If you don't have one yet, below is a roundup of suggestions to incorporate into your preparation routine. It doesn't matter whether you are climbing indoors or outdoors. These tips will help your body get ready for the actual climbing challenges.

Get Your Blood Circulating

Ten minutes of walking, jogging, running, or biking is enough to pump blood to your entire body while warming up your leg muscles at the same time. If you're planning outdoor climbing, walking or biking to the crag would be enough. If you're going indoor climbing, spend at least five minutes walking around inspecting various climbs or greeting fellow climbers.

Some light cardio exercises boost circulation and begin moving blood and oxygen to the different parts of your body, simultaneously storing them with the required fuel for your activity.

Loosen Up

The basic idea behind stretching requires holding a specific pose for about 15 to 30 seconds. However, recent sports science findings say that static stretching can, in fact, lessen muscle output. Rather than the static type, experts recommend **dynamic stretching with rotational movements** as it provides more advantages to muscles by building on the momentum to flexibility and imitating the kind of muscle strains during the climb.

Dynamic stretches lubricate the tendons and joints necessary to climbing, leading to increased muscle performance and reduced risk of injury. Meanwhile, static stretching can still be useful for a post-activity workout or rest days to supplement overall flexibility.

Here are some dynamic stretches you can try:

Walking Lunges

Walking lunges help you get your core and lower body moving and set to climb. To do this, you have to:

1. Keep your body in an upright position.

2. Step forward with one leg and gradually drop down into a lunge until your knee is merely a few inches off the ground.

3. As you stand back up, slowly step forward with the other leg, doing the same procedure in #2.

4. Repeat until you make 12 lunges on each leg.

Head Rolls

This exercise is particularly beneficial for steep climbers who usually crane their necks to look up and boulderers who usually fall and jar their necks and upper back. To perform head rolls, you need to:

1. Allow your head to relax forward wholly.

2. Slowly move it in a circular motion, both in a clockwise and counterclockwise direction. Ensure to keep your neck as loose as possible since the movement allows it to awaken tense muscles and align the vertebrae of your backbone to avoid injuries.

Side Twist Exercises

Side twist exercises are designed to strengthen your core and get rid of unnecessary belly fat. They benefit both the upper and lower abdominals plus the oblique muscles.

There are many side twists you can try on, but let us give you the Russian Twists, a full abdominal twist that involves strength, balancing, and isolation. It fixes the waist and reinforces the core.

Here's what you need to do:

1. Sit on an exercise mat with your knees bent and feet flat on the floor.
2. Lean back slightly and lift your feet off the floor. Put your hands on the mat for support if you must.
3. Once you find your balance, bring your hands together in front of you, with one hand cupping the other, and roll your shoulders back. Tighten your core and glutes—this form is your starting position.
4. Rotate your upper body to the left and touch the mat with your elbow. Be mindful of your form and balance, maintaining it for about five counts. Return to the starting position and twist to the right. This step completes one rep; do three sets of 12 repetitions each.

Windmill Exercise

The most commonly injured part of a climber's body is their shoulders. The windmill exercise focuses on your shoulder joints and helps pump blood to the forearm muscles and finger tissues.

1. Stand with your feet a bit wider than shoulder-width apart. Raise your right arm and leave your left hanging down on your side. Turn your left foot at a 90-degree angle, and look up at your right hand.
2. Tighten your core and push your hips to the right side, sliding your left hand down your left leg. Reach down as far as possible without placing too much pressure on your leg. Remember to use your core to stabilize yourself. Your

3. left arm should remain perpendicular to the ground. Your right leg should remain straight, while you can allow a minimal bend in your left leg to avoid locking your knee.
4. Hold the position and push down through your feet to rise back up to the start position. Keep your core tight and your spine straight the entire time.
5. Do 12 repetitions and switch sides.

Jump Squats

Many training plans incorporate squats simply because they serve as a universal workout for all the lower body muscles, particularly the legs. As you know, your legs are your body's climbing engine, and with this in mind, jump squats are appropriate to improve the power in your lower legs.

Warm Down

Rest is essential after doing warm-up exercises. Nonetheless, it would be best if you still were careful not to cool down too much, resulting in the much-feared flash pump. A ten-minute rest should be enough for boulderers who spend less time on the rock, while sport climbers should aim for about 15 minutes.

Body Training

Working out several times a week helps achieve the level of physical fitness your body needs for rock climbing. Having a clear schedule for regular training sessions also prepares your mind for the challenges you will experience during your endeavors.

But before we proceed to the main subject, let's go over some training tips:

*   Design your training program to be specific for rock climbing and enjoyable at the same time.
*   Organize a standard warm-up routine so that you can evaluate your feelings before starting a full-blown workout.
*   Systematically increase the number of exercises you do before heading to more intense training. Feel free to try out light, medium, and hard training periods for change.
*   The amount of time you spend on a workout is more critical than the amount of effort you should exert. For example, it's better to run a mile in 12 minutes than 8 minutes.

- Know when to work through your fatigue and when to stop before you completely exhaust yourself. Do not over-train and ensure that you have enough rest and time for recovery. You can also try different intervals between rest days and active days to determine what best suits you.
- Remember that working out to the point of complete exhaustion will lead to injury, reduced flexibility, and poor technique.
- Move around during your rest to maintain blood circulation and eliminate waste products from your muscle.
- Get a regular training partner or mentor to get you back on track whenever you feel motivated and give you the necessary feedback.

Here are the key points you must focus on:

Motor Fitness

Rock climbing is all about crags, walls, and terrain challenges. It's expected that anyone with this aspiration should develop their strength, endurance, power, and balance.

Strength and Power Training

Strength pertains to the ability "to hold on", while power refers to the ability "to move." Both are crucial during your rock-climbing project. You need leg strength as well as a strong core since you will be carrying a heavy load while ascending a cliff.

The principles of strength and power training for both the upper and lower bodies are pretty much the same. The training itself involves bodyweight routines and workouts that utilize traditional weights.

When you're trying to increase your strength and power, you can't train for a long time because your muscles can't bear it. So, pursue short, high-intensity exercises that will push your body to its limits.

Single-Arm Hang

A single-arm hang can help you increase functional strength, especially if one side of your body is weaker than the other. For example, people whose dominant hand is their right have a weak left side. Trying a single arm hang with your left arm will ameliorate this. You should perform three of the most typical hand positions for climbers: *open, full-crimp,* and *half-crimp.*

Steps:

1. Choose a hold, preferably the half-crimp grip position. If you're using loads, adjust it to the weight that will allow you to hang one-handed for 5 to 10 seconds.

2. Hang single-handedly for about 5 to 10 seconds in the slightly bent arm position. Repeat the hang using your other arm, then take a rest for about 2 to 5 minutes. Do a total of three hangs for each arm.

3. With your hand in a half-crimp grip position, hang single-handedly for about 5 to 10 seconds in the 90-degree bent arm position. Repeat this with the other arm, and rest for about 2 to 5 minutes. Do a total of three hangs for each arm.

4. With your hand in a half-crimp grip position, hang single-handedly for about 5 to 10 seconds in the full lock-off arm position. Repeat this with the other arm, and take a rest for about 2 to 5 minutes. Again, do a total of three hangs for each arm.

Pull-Ups

Another workout that can build your strength and power is pull-ups. Pull-ups have various styles, including *chin-ups, wide-hand,* and *close grip.* Each of these methods benefits your muscles a little bit distinctively, so you have to ensure that you're combining them well with your other exercises. Moreover, when you do pull-ups, try bursting up instead of doing the smooth-and-slow version. Doing this helps you achieve the maximum benefit of your workout regime.

Steps:

1. Begin by standing below a pull-up bar. Put your hands in an overhand grip, with palms facing away from you, at a distance of shoulder-width apart. Your arms and torso should form a "Y"— this is your starting position. *(Note: If you can't reach the bar from standing on the floor, feel free to use a sturdy box or footstool.)*

2. Breathe in and lift your feet from the ground so that you're hanging from the bar. Contract your trunk muscles as you pull your body upwards toward the bar until your chin is over the bar. Hold the position for a few seconds, avoiding swinging your legs all the while.

3. Breathe out as you bring your body back down in the starting position. Perform sets of 20 to 30 seconds with 1 to 2-minute intervals in between.

Push-Up with One-Hand Row Exercise

This workout trains your shoulders and arms, bolstering your upper-body strength for the ropework ahead.

Steps:

1. Start in a push-up position, with your hands on dumbbells and your feet shoulder-width apart.
2. **Lower your body down and push back up. Once you're back** up, row one elbow back, bringing the dumbbell up to the direction of your rib cage and returning it to the ground.
3. Perform another push-up and row the other elbow back, bringing the dumbbell up toward the rib cage then returning it to the ground.
4. Do 10 to 15 repetitions on each arm. Always maintain a plank position throughout the workout by keeping your body straight from head to toe. Keep your chin slightly tucked while looking at the ground.

Aside from these exercises, you can also try the following:

- Box jumps
- Clean (dumbbell clean and press and kettlebell clean)
- Medicine ball slams
- Medicine ball chest pass
- Muscle-up
- Snatches (kettlebell snatch, dumbbell power snatch, and hanging power snatch)

Whatever you choose for your strength and power training, always bear in mind to exercise with caution.

Preventing Injuries

If you're thinking that working out and building your skills and techniques are all there is to prepare for, then you're mistaken. When it comes to your safety, being proactive is also a significant part of the training.

As an individual whose passion is to reach summits, you are allowed to push your physical and mental boundaries, but not to the point of self-neglect. Prioritizing your health and safety is part of your responsibility. Here are some tips to follow.

- Always do warm-ups and stretches. Older climbers are also required a longer time for pre-climb warm-up and stretching.
- Consume lots of carbohydrates during heavy training. Always stay hydrated to avoid heat stress, sustain normal body function, and maintain performance levels.
- Do not forget to tape your fingers to avoid skin tears. Apply skin balms to help repair damaged skin on your hands.
- Never overdo training, especially when you feel worn out or sick. Take a rest at first signs of an injury.
- As a newbie, avoid executing extreme or complex moves. If a movement causes pain, don't do it.
- Remember that an increased amount of training requires an increased amount of rest.
- Remember to maintain the right balance between technique, strength and power, and endurance training.
- Modify your training sessions to prevent repetitive strains and keep them more exciting.

Training Myths to Watch Out For

Working out or training to climb, like many other things in this world, sometimes garner misconceptions like the following:

Pain is an Imperative in Training

Many people believe that training should hurt—it should NOT! Pain is an indication of an underlying issue, one that should never be ignored. Nevertheless, there will be discomfort because it's a natural result of muscle fatigue.

Trauma will Grant You Strength

In some sense, it might, but not when we're talking about MUSCLES. While some athletes experience muscle tear, that doesn't automatically equate to gained strength. In fact, bruised muscles will need four to six weeks to recover from significant tearing of the tissues.

Furthermore, some people erroneously believe that you have to push your body to the breaking point in order to unlock your next-level potential. While this may be beneficial at times, particularly in power training, the body cannot heal properly if this happens in every session. Plus, this form of self-inflicted torture will harm not only your body but your mind, too.

Muscles will Turn into Fats

While muscles may decrease when one reduces their training, it doesn't mean that these specialized cells will turn into fats. Fats will only increase when a person overeats.

Lactic Acid will Cause Soreness

Lactic acid dwindles within an hour after a workout. Afterward, any soreness you experience is due to muscle trauma and swelling. To reduce this, you can try squeezing a softball or jogging after the training.

Balance Training

Balance exercises focus on how to increase body awareness and boost your ability to deal with complicated terrains while you're loaded with a heavy rucksack. For your training, you will have to incorporate both *static* and *dynamic* exercises as these contribute massively to the development of this fitness skill.

Static balance exercises are pretty straightforward that you can even practice them at home. Here's another simple one:

Cardiovascular Fitness

Cardio training consists of both aerobic exercises and interval training. Each session is crucial to boost the overall fitness level of both your heart and lungs. It should be the first type of training you work on for your preparation since it's the foundation for your ability to climb for long periods.

Aerobic Training

The aerobic exercises can be as follows:

- Jump rope
- Speed walking
- Running
- Biking
- Swimming
- Climbing and descending stairs, stadium bleachers, or hills
- Hiking

Improve your aerobic training gradually, starting with shorter sessions then intensifying it with longer workouts. Your target is to feel confident with an aerobic exertion at the level of your daily climb activities. Consider the preparation for the downhill climb as well. You can try training on different terrains and developing your aerobic capacity for the descent.

Longer hikes and treks will also help you develop your abilities for the exhausting days of your climbing project. Nothing will prepare you for doing extensive training.

The frequency of your aerobic training is up to you. You can train every day if you like, but make sure not to overdo it because it will end up hurting you instead of benefiting you. Also, include some rest intervals each week.

Experts highly recommend 30-minute aerobic training per session, intending to keep your training range at about 65% to 85% of your maximum heart rate. You can calculate your maximum heart rate based on your age. All you need to do is to deduct your age from 220. So, if you're 35 years old, your maximum heart rate is 185. That is:

$$220 - 35 = 185 \text{ beats per minute}$$

Therefore, your training range should stay between 120 to 157 beats per minute. This is the general formula one can use for training, but still, you should be conscious of how you feel. Your perceived exertion provides you a better signal of how you should be performing on a given day. After all, we have good days and bad days—this is how your perception will help you decide on things.

Interval Training

Interval training is another essential factor in boosting your cardiovascular base and climbing preparation. Keep in mind that as you ascend, altitude increases while atmospheric pressure decreases. When this happens, you get less oxygen with each breath.

Interval training is designed to improve your capability to utilize oxygen. As such, the sessions involve a set of reps of high-intensity aerobic exercises executed at a faster pace than your usual workouts. These exercises are distributed to accommodate low-intensity recovery exercises in between sequences.

This type of workout also maximizes your cardio benefits, helping your heart become stronger while building on your anaerobic capacity. You can further develop your ability to work at a variety of paces.

During the rest periods, you can recover your energy and enhance your general performance with surge training.

You can obtain the most benefits of your interval training for a period of three months. Also, you have to do these every three days in your schedule.

Experts suggest that climbers should include these activities in their interval training:

- Running intervals or slow jogging (5 minutes)
- Time-trial cycling (30 minutes)
- Speed hiking (up to 60 minutes)

Calf Raises with Ball

This exercise improves weight-shifting and push-off onto footholds. It benefits the posterior tibialis and gastrocnemius muscles.

Steps:

1. Place a basketball between your legs, just above your ankles.

2. Raise your heels, transferring your weight right on your big toes.

3. Hold the position for about 5 to 10 seconds before bringing your heels down.

4. Perform 10 to 15 sets.

Why not try doing some yoga poses like what we have here below?

The Tree Pose

This yoga pose helps engage core muscles to support alignment from head to foot. You can modify this exercise by resting your heel against the standing ankle or doing the pose on tiptoe.

Steps:

1. Start in a standing position and feet should be hip-width apart, with your hands by your sides and palms facing forward.
2. Start to move your weight onto the right foot and bend your left knee.
3. Slowly hold your left ankle with your left hand, placing your left foot sole against your inner right thigh (or leg). 1. Your toes should point towards the ground.
4. Engage your core as you position your palms together in a prayer pose. Face forward and hold your breath for about two to three seconds before putting your left foot back down on the ground.
5. Repeat the steps on the other side.
6. Do ten sets per side.

Single-Leg Warrior

In this exercise, you don't have to force your back leg to be lifted super high. You can begin with a lower lift while maintaining your spine straight. You can also bend your standing leg slightly to achieve a more grounding effect.

Steps:

1. Start in a lunge position by stepping your right foot behind you. It should land on the ball of your foot. Bend your left knee in front, pressing your left foot against the ground. Ensure that your right knee never touches the ground.
2. Simultaneously strengthen your left leg as you raise your right foot behind you. It should be aligned with your hips and back, making it parallel to the floor. Keep your right foot flexed. In order not to ruin your balance, try to straighten your left leg.
3. Put your palms together in a prayer pose and hold the position for about two to three seconds.

4. Bring your right foot back down and stand straight.
5. Repeat the steps for the other side.
6. Do ten sets per side.

You can also try static exercises with equipment like dumbbells:

One-Leg Deadlift

This exercise engages your core muscles and hips to enhance both strength and balance as you concentrate your weight over each side of your body. To modify this, you can adjust how far you bend toward the ground and use a heavier or lighter dumbbell.

Steps:

1. For your starting position, hold a dumbbell with your left hand while standing straight with your feet shoulder-width apart.
2. Focus your weight over your right foot, then bend forward at the hips, slowly extending your left or right leg backward. Make sure to maintain your balance with your back straight as you take the dumbbell down toward the ground.
3. Return to the starting position while engaging your core and glutes. Ensure that your back remains straight throughout.
4. Perform a set of 20 before switching to your other side; do another set of 20.
5. Dynamic exercises involve standing, moving around, and stepping from one place to another. The simplest one is by walking forward in a straight line, focusing on each step from heel to toe. And then, walk backward to the starting point. You can level this exercise up by doing it with your eyes closed.

Other dynamic exercises and activities that can help improve your balance include:

- Running in a zigzag line
- Running with crossovers
- Stair climbing
- Stepping over obstacles
- Playing racquet sports such as tennis, table tennis, and badminton
- Roller skating or ice skating

Endurance Training

Like balance and strength, endurance is a motor skill that you can further develop with proper training. In a nutshell, endurance training focuses on persistently intensifying your workout and not being content with your current routine or fitness level. Training this way can help you achieve a more sturdy physique that allows you to climb more efficiently over long hours while helping you adapt to unexpected challenges you encounter on the course of your climb.

As a beginner, your priority is to build your endurance. You can start with the following exercises.

Step-Up Exercise

This exercise bolsters both strength and endurance in your quad muscles and glutes so that you can keep on going up the cliffs and crags for many hours. You will need a training box or any stable surface elevated about eight inches from the ground. You will also have to wear a weighted backpack, beginning with about 10 pounds. You will add more pounds as you progress each week.

Steps:

- Do the starting position by placing your left foot on the ground and your right on the top of the step.
- Step up until you're standing with your right leg, making sure that your left foot is slightly bent so that it doesn't touch the platform. Hold this position for about two to three seconds before stepping down with your left leg and then your right leg.
- Repeat it 15 times before switching to the other side.

The Mountain Climber Exercise

This exercise focuses on your core and develops your leg work.

Steps:

- Begin with your body in a plank position, with straight arms at the top of a pushup.
- Move your right knee as close as you can to your right elbow.
- Keep your hips in line with your back, head, and feet. Avoid arching your back; keep it flat throughout the exercise.
- Bring your leg to the starting position and bring your left leg towards your left elbow.
- Repeat these steps quickly; do sets from 20 to 60 seconds, depending on your ability.

Walking Lunges With KB or DB

This exercise utilizes weights— kettlebells or dumbbells. It will test you in various ways but will teach your body endurance and stability. Aside from the equipment, you will also need about a 10-meter space in front of you for this workout.

Steps:

- Hold the kettlebells or dumbbells; stand straight and look ahead.
- Take a forward step with your right leg--with your heel first then the ball of your foot.
- Lower your body, allowing your left knee to touch the floor
- Stand on your right leg with the assistance of your left leg.
- Lunge forward with your left leg.
- Repeat the alternating lunges. Make sure that your hands, which are holding the weights, do not sway as you lunge.
- Repeat 10-12 on each leg; perform two to three sets.

Aside from these exercises, it is recommended for you to practice indoor climbing for 30-minute periods. It is one way to build your endurance in climbing effectively.

You may choose a route or two to work on or routes that require simple-to-moderate movements that you feel comfortable with. Keep climbing for 30 minutes with no rest. Continuous movement during this practice is a perfect way to hone your technique and endurance.

Chapter 6: Safety Checks

Safety checking, especially in rock climbing, is a critical component of any preparation. After setting up for the climb, you need to check everything to ensure safety thoroughly. Avoiding shortcuts is strongly recommended. Any human can sustain a 10-feet fall, but what about if you fall from a height of 60-100 feet?

When rock climbing or mountaineering, you can't do without not having a climbing buddy. One needs a belayer so that in case of a fall, you won't fall very far. The belayer is also responsible for decreasing or increasing the rope friction and providing you with more rope to continue climbing.

Safety Checking

Here's how to conduct a safety check.

- Remove all unnecessary things like rings, watches, necklaces, bracelets, for there's a big possibility that these items can snag rock features as you climb or fall. There are reported incidents involving snagging, and they are particularly gruesome and painful.
- The next step is to check that you and your belayer's harnesses are appropriately secured. See to it that all buckles are double-backed in three places - waist and both legs. Also, ensure the belay loop and cross piece or that webbing connecting leg loops, belay loop, and finally, to your waistline. Make sure that the leg loops aren't twisted.
- Once you are ready to tie in, tie yourself using the figure-8 rewoven knot.

If you are not skillful with your knot, ask your belayer to help you. It is also the responsibility of your belayer to double-check your tie-in knot.

If you happen to be the belayer, always ensure that you have correctly set up your gear.

- The carabiner must be securely clipped in the belay loop
- Check for any twisting in the belay rope
- The rope must be inserted correctly in the belay device and looped through the carabiner.
- Also, make sure to clip the carabiner through the rope bright and not only the belay device's wire guide.
- Check on the rope to see if it is correctly oriented

- Lock the carabiner gate to secure the system.

As both the climber and the carabiner should check on each other's safety, it is best to have a third party double-check on both of them.

Top Roping Preparation

When lead climbers had set up the top rope, they untied their knots and pulled one end of the rope down for the other end to come up. This way, the next in line won't wildly swing if they fall.

Spotting

Never underestimate the cliff. Always think of safety as many accidents happen on the first few feet of the crag.

When you're about to climb or in routes prone to a pendulum fall, a climber must have a spotter -- a person whose responsibility is to direct the climber's body to the ground during a fall so they can land safely on the ground.

A spotter position is directly behind and below the climber with knees bent slightly and legs apart. To spot, you have to position your arms up with a slight bend at the elbows, palms facing outward, and fingers pointing upward.

So as the climber scrambles upward to hold, raise your arms, placing your palm near their hips or torso in case of a fall, you can quickly grip their hips and steer them towards the ground.

Basic Communication

Basic Commands

The success and safety of a climb depend mainly on effective communication between the belayer and the climber. In the sport of rock climbing, short and simple commands are easier to understand and execute, but in crags where there are other climbers and belayers, make sure that you correctly address it to the person you're communicating by including their name at the end of the command. It will prevent confusion and also make sure that the person you're referring to can properly hear you by speaking in a loud voice.

Basic commands that are commonly used in top-roping are:

STARTING COMMANDS		
Command	**Given**	**From – To**
On belay?	Am I on belay? Am I secured?	Climber to belayer
On belay!	I'm ready! You are secured! I'm ready to take your fall.	Belayer to climber
Climbing!	I'm going to climb now!	Climber to belayer
Climb on!	An go ahead and climb	Belayer to Climber
COMMANDS ON THE ROCK		
Slack!	The rope is too tight! Loosen it a bit.	Climber to belayer
Slacking!	I'm loosening the rope a bit!	Belayer to climber

Tension! Take!	Pull the rope tight	Climber to belayer
Taking!	I'm pulling the rope tight	Belayer to climber
Watch me!	Pay attention! I'm going to make a move, and I may fall!	Climber to belayer
Go ahead!	I'm ready. Make the move	Belayer to climber
Falling!	I'm going to fall! The belayer must pay close attention. Most falls suddenly happen, and the climber may not have the time to shout this command!	Climber to belayer
Gotcha!	Don't worry. I'm stopping your fall! I'm ready to take your fall	Belayer to climber
Ready to Lower!	I've reached the anchor! I can't climb up anymore! You need to lower me down!	Climber to belayer

Lowering!	I'm going to lower you down now!	Belayer to climber
Rock!	Look out! Something is falling, and it might hit you!	Climber to belayer
Rope!	Stay Clear! I'm pulling down a rope.	Climber to belayer

Master these basic commands as they can save either your life or that of your belayer.

Proper Belaying Technique

When belaying a climber or climbers, it means that they are entrusting to you their lives -- and this is speaking.

A belayer's responsibility is to keep the climber safe while climbing. With such a big responsibility on your hand, you must know how to perform belaying properly. Because life is at stake, you have to understand that your task is so critical.

Having focus at all times is an essential quality required for a belayer. You have to focus on the climber and don't allow anyone or anything to distract you. When climbing, think of nothing else but the climber before you, for you will never know when a wrong step could suddenly cause their fall. Don't be complacent, and a lapse in concentration can be everything.

When belaying, ensure that the carabiner is not cross-loaded - meaning, the carabiner's gate is taking the load. It happens when the carabiner shifts and the gate or spine side of the carabiner ends up crossing the rope or the belay loop, as this is the weakest point of the carabiner.

A carabiner is intended to be explicitly loaded in its long axis at the bends, above and below the spine. In other directions, it is weak, and the gate is considered the weakest point. It might easily snap off if shock-loaded under the weight and stress of a falling climber.

So, from time to time, a belayer must check the carabiner to ensure that it's not cross-loaded. Also, ensure that all attachment points are at the major axis of the carabiner.

For a proper belay stance, put your feet forward to gain balance against the climber's weight. If you are right-handed, your right hand will serve as your brake hand, and your left hand will be your guide hand. Conversely, left-handed individuals have dominant left hands. Therefore, their left hands are the brake hands.

Steps in Proper Belaying

Here are proper steps to observe when belaying.

Step #1:

- Take hold of the climber's rope with your guide hand.
- Grip the brake end of the rope with your brake hand - or the remaining rope that leads to your coil.
- See to it that your brake hand must never leave the rope.

Step #2: While the climber starts to climb, the rope creates slack, and you have to pull that slack out using your hand guide. With your brake hand, pull the slack through.

Slack #3: Bring your brake hand to your hip to lock the rope in case of a climber's fall.

Step # 4: Bring your guide hand around and above your brake hand, slightly behind the belay device. Some opt to place their guide hand right under the brake hand rather than over their brake hand. It is also a safe technique.

What Must a Belayer Do in Case of a Fall?

In case of an accident causing a climber to fall off the cliff, the belayer must quickly lock the rope as described in Step #3 to stop the fall. To block the fall, position your brake hand on or just a little behind your hip.

The belayer must concentrate on the climber and not allow any form of distraction to get his focus away from the climber. However, the belayer may converse with others around them but must not take their eyes off the climber.

As much as possible, spectators must avoid talking to the belayer while in action to prevent losing their focus on the climber.

As soon as the climber reaches the peak of the route, the belayer must lower them down. In lowering, the belayer takes up all the slack and positions their brake hand on the hip. They then place their guide hand near and behind the belay device.

When the climber is ready for the lowering, the belayer will bend their knees a little to counter the climber's weight, then gently ease up the brake hand on the rope to reduce friction. They then guide the rope to the belay device with the guiding hand and continue doing it until the climber safely reaches the ground.

Chapter 7: Transition to Outdoor Climbing

Climbing gyms have their reputation as excellent places if you are looking for an enjoyable workout or want to have some fun doing physical fitness.

However, pulling on plastic holds and beating your climbing routine in your local gym could lead to boredom in the long run as you get accustomed to them.

For this reason, the idea of transitioning to outdoor climbing attracts many gym climbers who desire the taste of a new challenge.

But then outdoor climbing is more challenging than a gym where you might have been practicing daily your climbing routines and where you are already familiar with the walls you scale.

On the other hand, an outdoor climb requires excellent skills, loads of gears, and a solid head on top of everything. It's not guaranteed that the local crag will be very easy for you if you are good at the climbing gym. It could be quite far from what you expect. Therefore, it would be best to approach it with high respect. Also, learn new techniques, and find an experienced mentor to guide you.

How to Start Outdoor Rock Climbing

Look for a guide or ask an experienced friend in rock climbing to go with you. It will help if you have an expert guide because climbing outdoors entails a higher level of risk for climbers.

Remember that the local crags and mountains are dangerous because they are exposed to rain, snow, and temperature change. Your decision to climb outdoors also depends on the location and season of the year.

Books or other literary information about DIY outdoor climbing can be helpful, but getting an experienced, professional guide will significantly lessen your risk of danger.

Climbing gyms can also offer great outdoor climbing resources if you don't have an experienced buddy to go with you.

Furthermore, numerous gyms offer outdoor climbing classes. REI of the USA provides outdoor school classes, and there's Glenmoor Lodge and Plas Y Brenin in the UK. You may browse the internet for a certified guide school or professional guide to take you in for classes. They can be beneficial if you want a personal outdoor climbing experience.

As for the cost of climbing lessons, most guided lessons and classes will cost you a large sum (most often, hundreds of dollars). Unless you have a willing outdoor climbing buddy, learning outdoors via climbing classes will not be accessible to you. But then, it would be advisable to repay them with a six-pack because teaching someone how to climb outdoors is a great deal of work. You couldn't possibly learn it for a week because outdoor climbing requires a repeated practice of different skills that will equip you until you are competent enough to go out alone.

Lastly, you can ask the climbing r gym where you are a member if they offer discounts on their classes -- and most of them do.

Necessary Gears for Climbing

Though your local gym may consider you to be lead certified, top-roping is essential for outdoor climbing. Also, expect that you are the one to buy your rope and set it up yourself when you climb outdoors, unlike in the gym, where top ropes are already in place.

At first, your friend or guide school will provide the gear that you are going to use. However, you will need to buy yours, so you can start practicing your skills like anchor building, tying knots, and rope management even at the comfort of your home.

Also, it is advisable not to borrow climbing gears due to serious safety reasons - you can't be sure about the actual condition of the gear unless you're the only one who is using it.

Skills You Need to Learn

To master outdoor top-roping skills, go with a professional outdoor climber. You may have already known these fundamental skills if you are a gym climber, but if not, equip yourself with these skills first:

- Figure-eight knot tying
- Double fisherman's knot tying
- Belaying
- Lowering off a climb

Other new skills specific to outdoor climbing that you need to learn:

- Top rope anchor building
- Top rope hanging
- Rope management
- Safety elements, especially backing yourself up at the anchors.

Rappelling is also required if the layout of the climbing area calls for it.

Gym Ratings vs. Outdoor Ratings

As mentioned earlier, the outdoor climb is not the same as climbing gyms, where routes are more leniently graded than outdoor climbing guides. If you can climb 5.12 in the gym, don't expect to get it right away when outdoors.

If you're the competitive type, you might get a little disappointed about grades as an outdoor newbie-oclimber. Don't take it too seriously. Focus on your skills and develop them. Master new movements you will need when facing natural rocks.

Outdoor climbing is a different world outside the experience of climbing gyms. You may spend a few hours in the gym, but outdoor climbing could take all day, which means you must have greater endurance to finish the task. You can take breaks in between routes and make sure to warm up or cool yourself down. Top it all up by having fun. After all, you wouldn't go rock climbing if not for fun, would you?

Other Things to Consider When Mountain Climbing

Mental Fitness

Indoor climbing requires the climber to face their fear of heights and falling, but you will indeed be tested in various ways with outdoor climbing.

- No colored holds for route marks. It would help if you found your way by trying different techniques and movements until you unlock a sequence.
- You must trust your partner and gear more.
- Prepare yourself for scrapes and bruises when you start to try developing your outdoor climbing skills. Natural rock won't give you mercy.
- Your hands may take a beating. Granite, limestone, and gritstone are textured and can be sharp, unlike plastic gym holds.

Climbing in the gym will undoubtedly train you to face your fear of heights and test your self-esteem. However, when climbing outdoors, the most complex challenge would be the lack of visual direction on the face of a gigantic rock, plus the trust that you have in your buddy, gear, and gear placements.

Climbing a natural rock can leave bruises and scrapes on your skin without you even feeling them. If you think you have those blisters at the gym because of those plastic holds, they are nothing compared to what you will get when you're climbing outdoors.

Not only will outdoor climbing challenge you physically, but nature also has its way of wreaking havoc on your mind and senses. While climbing to the top or hanging on the cliff, you can't help but ponder on terrifying thoughts like:

What if my fingertips fail to grip that tiny thing of the ledge suddenly breaks when I grab it?

Terrifying as it seems, it's what makes rock climbing more exciting and fun than any outdoor sports or hobby. By learning its fundamentals, you can challenge yourself in ways you never thought possible, and with much effort and endurance, you can overcome it.

First Aid or Emergency Kit

It's a great thing to have your first aid kit with you at all times, mainly because of the outdoors' nature. Your kit should include these items:

- Blister care
- Ibuprofen
- Band-aids
- Alcohol wipes
- Bandage or gauze

You can also check out online articles and tips on building a simple first aid kit for climbers.

Nutrition and Hydration

Since outdoor activity takes longer, bring plenty of water, snacks, and lunch so you won't get hungry or dehydrated. Bring caloric snacks like energy bars or trail mix because climbing can use up a lot of your energy.

Fill up your bottle with water - bring as much as you can to hydrate yourself for the whole day. Don't expect a drinking fountain waiting at the top of your climb.

Handling the Elements

Last but surely not least, check these elements:

- Check the weather before you go for an outdoor climb.
- Rocks would be wet if it rained in the past week. It will take a few days before they dry out completely and are no longer slippery.
- Pack your sunglasses, hat, and sunscreen if the weather is hot or sunny.
- Always bring your jacket. You can't be sure that it will not rain.
- Wear clothes appropriate for the day's temperature.

Indeed, gyms are also great places to climb for training purposes and when the weather is not suitable for outdoor climbing. But still, when it comes to experience with natural rock, outdoor climbing is unbeatable. So, use the above tips to plan your first trip and have fun with outdoor climbing.

Chapter 8: Advancing Climbing Skills

If you intend to make progress on your climbing skills, then train seriously. It is necessary to understand the importance of training to develop your technical, physical, and mental abilities. After you have mastered your basic techniques, it's time to work on advanced skills to increase efficacy. This chapter will deal with some rock climbing skills to help you advance your climbing skills, particularly in footwork, balancing, and more advanced climbing moves.

Aim for More Climbs

If you want improvements in your climbing skills, the best way to do it is to do it consistently. There are ways to practice climbing in different styles so you can continue to develop your skill, strength, and technique, regardless of where you are. There's no shortcut to this, as experience is always the best teacher.

Do not spend too much time on physical training. It's only in actual climbing that you can develop your technique. Set your goal for days—either on the rock or gym, and allow adequate rest and recovery. When you're climbing more than ever, only then can you expect some improvements.

Newbie climbers often rely more on their buddies or group. It won't help you improve if you go with the flow. Instead, have your plan and objective. So before you go, check your local guidebook or the location that you want to explore. Choose a few options for warming up and have an idea of the routes you want to try. You can pick climbs that look cool and within your comfort zone, but remember to choose a couple of routes that could challenge and optimize your climbing conditions.

Check for details and determine if you want to expose yourself to the sun or the shade.

There's only one way to achieve your full potential, and that is by pushing yourself to reach your optimal level. It also means working on your weaknesses. So, if you're comfortable with vertical climbs and you want to get better, jump on some deep steep routes, too. Suppose you are scared of some climbing style so that you are avoiding them. Chances are, you are missing some learning opportunities.

Make an Effort to Learn

Fear is one factor that deprives most climbers of achieving optimum performance. It is natural to be scared of things you haven't experienced before. Even the boldest climbers need to deal with their fear of falling. However, you have to learn how to go against your natural survival instincts. Knowing how to handle your fear can make a big difference.

There are many ways to overcome your fear, and one is to gradually get out of your comfort zone. To do it, most climbers would practice falling.

Look for an overhanging route with a solid anchor. Ensure that you bring with you a belayer. Start by taking a few falls on the top rope, and when you're ready to lead, climb a little above the bolt and then take a shortfall. Move up higher above your last bolt to practice more significant falls.

Eventually, you will gain more confidence as you master the art of falling and not just climbing.

Redpointing, or the act of climbing a route clean after some attempts and practice, takes time, dedication, and strategy. Climbing can be daunting, just like when you're trying to achieve a goal. However, the plan is to break down a massive chunk into smaller pieces. If you find the goal too challenging to achieve, break it down into smaller objectives, so it can be easy to work on it. The same method works for rock climbing. Breaking down the climb piece by piece makes it less overwhelming.

If those chances of falling intimidate you, then practice the route on the top route. Go to the top of the cliff to hang the rope, or you may also be able to reach the anchors from an adjacent route. If you have someone strong as your climbing buddy, let them roe-gun for you.

Once you are ready to try lead climbing, you can start to tackle the route bolt by bolt and take a rest after each cliff. We call such a technique hang dogging. It allows you to feel out the moves with a clear head and fresher arms. Never hesitate to pull through tricky areas, for it might be possible to clip a draw overhead and then pull on it to go through a crux section.

You can adopt strategies to make clipping easy and with a better flow while helping you save your energy.

As long as no other climbers are waiting on the route, first, leave your quickdraws in place between attempts. If a route has a tricky clip, it will be easier to clip from a safer stance by using a long sling or linking dog bones together.

And lastly, always give it another try!

A climb may seem challenging at first, but as you gain more experience, you can quickly figure out the moves and link sequences.

Advanced Climbing Techniques

Great climbers apply techniques to their way up to the top using moves designed to help them attack specific problems. If you intend to become a better climber, you have to hone your technique and movement, and the excellent way to do it is to climb every opportunity you have. Improving techniques involves mastering principles of balance and movements, and then you can concentrate on nailing the nuances of individual moves.

It's hard not to emphasize the significance of good technique in rock climbing. For once you focus on strategy, your moves start to click in place, and you'll find yourself floating up routes that seemed too difficult before.

Now, let's cover three essential climbing techniques which are significant to advancing your climbing skills.

Footwork Technique

Footwork is the foundation of climbing. Beginners in climbing tend to pull themselves up to the wall and quickly tire out. It's not easy fighting gravity pull this way. Let's say we are climbing a ladder. Are you pulling yourself up to climb every step? Of course not! You have to step up and use your arms and hands for balance. It's the same thing with climbing.

The basic climbing footwork you use in climbing is edging and smearing.

When climbing, remember the following footwork techniques.

- Have your feet directly below you, and to maintain your balance, keep an eye out for footholds in good positions.

- Prioritize searching for placements over handholds.
- Once you have your foot set, keep it still. You have a better chance of staying on hold as you proceed to your next move.

To have plenty of contact with the wall, keep your heel low. With your heel high, less rubber is in touch with the rock, reducing friction. It also increases the odds of levering your foot off the wall when making the next move.

Balancing Technique

Climbing is pretty intuitive when you are lucky enough to have a line of jugs leading straight up the wall. But when you're on a route where you need to move and pull in different directions, you have to use your body to maintain balance.

When you need to use a hold out to the side, you can't pull straight down. Therefore, you have to find a way to counter the force of that side pull. This way, you won't be losing your balance and barn-door off the wall.

Balancing Strategies

- Create counter pressure by pressing your foot in the opposite direction of the pull
- With your other hand on a hooked foot, pull in the opposite direction.
- Use your body weight by leaning over hard enough to provide balance.

Efficient Climbing Tips

A great way to a successful rock climbing is by learning how to save energy and relieve your muscles of tension as you climb.

Here are some efficient climbing tips.

- Straight arms allow your bones to take most of the weight and give your muscles a break.
- Try to concentrate on your hips. Beginners tend to keep their hips squared to the wall, which provides them a sense of stability. However, this action pushes your weight away from the wall and stresses your muscles.
- Keeping one hip pushed up against the wall can help distribute your weight on your feet, allowing you to lean back with straight arms

- With a hip close to the wall, it brings your shoulder closer, and with your weight over your feet, it decreases the chances of peeling off. A close shoulder likewise changes the angle of the pull-on handholds, providing you with an easier grip.
- Good climbers keep their eyes on the wall, searching for holds that let them take a quick rest. Don't just be concerned with chalk marks.
- Use a good rest when you find it. Allow your heart rate to slow down and give your arms a shake to improve circulation.

Advanced Climbing Moves

There are some advanced climbing techniques you can develop to work your way up between rests to help you save energy. Here are some of them.

Advanced Rock-Over

If you have developed your flexibility, you can now try to place your foot beside your hand into a rock-over. This advanced technique is beneficial for short and hard slabs. Build up slowly as this move puts a strain on your groin.

Stand side on when making a move, and you will be able to step through onto the outside edge of your foot. Alternate stepping to zigzag upward with both your left and right foot.

Dyno

The Dyno move requires a good amount of energy and vibrancy, which is why many climbers consider this an insane action.

If the next hold is too far to reach, climbers use the dyno move to stretch their hands and keep their hips closer to the wall, a quick leap to grab the handhold. It is pretty scary and fun. Only those who are advanced in their climbing lessons can execute it. Before you can perform this movement successfully, it requires core strength, control, and precision. You have to leap to grab the hold, and your grip must be extra vital as the momentum your body creates from the jump makes it hard for you to contain strength.

Bat-Hang

Here is one underrated technique in climbing—the bat-hang. Only a few high-ranking climbers can perform this move. You hang upside down from the wall like a bat, using only your toes, as the name implies.

There must be a steep wall with a hold large enough to accommodate both feet to do the bat-hang technique. Position the edge of the hold right above your toe joints and position your legs perpendicularly with your toes and feet. They must be straight and tense.

Climbers would use the bat-hang to rest their arms, and when they are in a position where they must climb through a jug with feet first before grabbing the next hold with their hand.

Slopers

Slopers are big, round, and inclined holds that a climber can easily find in a natural setting. It requires precision along with careful distribution of body weight.

Friction is significant to sloping that best climbers had to chalk well before performing this technique.

In sloping, climbers would place their forehands on the holds with forearms straight, and fingers close together for more strength.

There are more climbing moves that you need to master as you progress in your rock climbing endeavor. The bottom line here is not to stop learning and continue to gain more experience as you learn.

Leave a 1-click review!

Customer Reviews

★★★★★ 2
5.0 out of 5 stars ▾

5 star		100%
4 star		0%
3 star		0%
2 star		0%
1 star		0%

Share your thoughts with other customers

Write a customer review

See all verified purchase reviews ›

I would be incredibly grateful if you take just 60 seconds to write just a brief review on Amazon, even if it's just a few sentences.

https://www.amazon.com/review/create-review-asin=B09MLQHCL3

Conclusion

Rock climbing has become an adventure sport and recreation for many adrenaline lovers and sports enthusiasts for the past decades. The challenges it brings along with the dangers and health benefits might be a part of the appeal of rock climbing, but many climbers believe that what is alluring about it is its mental and physical requirements. More than the physical ability, rock climbing requires clear and positive thinking to keep you safe at all times.

Rock climbing can even be more challenging for beginners. However, by learning more about the types, methods, and safety precautions, you may choose the best one for you and avoid the danger it entails.

Rock climbing is also one activity that reconnects you to nature and heightens your awareness of wildlife and your responsibility in maintaining our ecology.

Lastly, because of the dangers involved in rock climbing, it requires you to develop survival skills necessary when facing any crisis, and not only limited to the sport or activity itself.

Now that you have armed yourself with the knowledge and right tools to participate in rock climbing activities, don't hesitate to use them. If you find this book enjoyable to read, please leave a review on Amazon.

My other books you will love!

Amazon.com/dp/B09MMCN3X8

Amazon.com/dp/B09MMDPFKT

Don't forget to grab your GIFT!!!

Visit this link

https://www.samaconnelly.com/perfect-adventure.pdf

Joining the WA Community

Looking to live your dreams by having the best adventures and meeting other fun lovers like you? If so, then check out the Wild Adventurers (WA) Community here:

https://www.facebook.com/groups/173808284952610/

References

The 7 Principles - Leave No Trace Center for Outdoor Ethics. (2021, March 17). Retrieved from https://lnt.org/why/7-principles/

A. (2021a, June 27). How to Actually Get Better at Climbing. Retrieved from https://www.outsideonline.com/health/training-performance/how-to-rock-climb-better-tips-principles/

A. (2021b, August 24). The Complete Guide to Rock Climbing Training, 5 Lessons. Retrieved from https://www.climbing.com/skills/learn-to-train-a-complete-guide-to-climbing-training/

Aleksey, A. (2018, October 15). Types of Rock Climbing. - International Rock Climbing School. Retrieved November 9, 2021, from https://climbingschool.org/types-of-climbing

Ellis, A. (2020, February 23). How to Transition from Indoor to Outdoor Climbing. Retrieved from https://www.theclimbingguy.com/transition-to-outdoor-climbing/

Holmes, J. (2020, October 27). 63 Useful Rock Climbing Terms Every Climber Should Know. Retrieved from https://coolofthewild.com/rock-climbing-terms/

Locke, A. (2016a, July 22). How to Make the Transition from Indoor to Outdoor Rock Climbing. Retrieved from https://www.theoutbound.com/amber-locke/how-to-make-the-transition-from-indoor-to-outdoor-rock-climbing

Locke, A. (2016b, July 22). How to Make the Transition from Indoor to Outdoor Rock Climbing. Retrieved from https://www.theoutbound.com/amber-locke/how-to-make-the-transition-from-indoor-to-outdoor-rock-climbing

Madness, M. (2020, April 10). Climbing Rating Systems. Retrieved from https://mountainmadness.com/resources/climbing-rating-systems

National PArk Service. (2021, May 28). Types of Climbing - Climbing (U.S. National Park Service). Retrieved November 9, 2021, from https://www.nps.gov/subjects/climbing/types-of-climbing.htm

P. (n.d.). Everything You Need to Know About Mountaineering. Retrieved from https://www.flypgs.com/en/extreme-sports/mountaineering

RMI Expeditions. (n.d.). Training for Mountaineering | RMI Expeditions. Retrieved from https://www.rmiguides.com/resources/fitness-and-training

SARL Undiscovered Mountains France. (2020, April 15). Mountaineering Training - Everything You Need to Know When Training for a Climb. Retrieved November 9, 2021, from https://undiscoveredmountains.com/mountaineering-training-everything-you-need-to-know-when-training-for-a-climb?utm_source=pocket_mylist

Sein, L. (2021, July 30). How to Progress in Rock Climbing - 10 Tips for Beginners. Retrieved from https://outdoorswithnolimits.com/how-to-progress-in-rock-climbing-10-techniques-for-beginners-that-work/

Sheila, G. A. (2018, March 2). Rock Climbing 101: Safety Checks, Communication, and Proper Belaying Technique. Retrieved from https://adrenalineromance.com/2013/04/11/rock-climbing-safety-checks/

Staff, R. (2015, June 17). Climbing partner safety checks. Retrieved from https://rockclimbeveryday.com/climbing-partner-safety-checks/

Staff, R. (2020a, September 18). How to Tie Climbing Knots, Hitches and Bends. Retrieved from https://www.rei.com/learn/expert-advice/climbing-knots.html

Staff, R. (2020b, September 18). How to Train for Mountaineering. Retrieved from https://www.rei.com/learn/expert-advice/mountaineering-how-to-cross-train.html

Staff, R. (2020c, September 18). Rock Climbing Glossary. Retrieved from https://www.rei.com/learn/expert-advice/rock-climbing-glossary.html

Time Outdoors. (n.d.). Training for Climbing for Beginners. Retrieved from https://www.timeoutdoors.com/expert-advice/climbing/beginners/training-for-climbing

Undiscovered Mountain. (2020, April 15). Mountaineering Training - Everything You Need to Know When Training for a Climb. Retrieved from https://undiscoveredmountains.com/mountaineering-training-everything-you-need-to-know-when-training-for-a-climb